ALL THE BEST STIR-FRIES

ALL   THE   BEST

STIR-FRIES

B Y
JOIE WARNER

HEARST BOOKS • New York

A FLAVOR BOOK

LIBRARY OF CONGRESS CATALOGING-IN-PUBLICATION DATA
Warner, Joie.
  All the best stir-fries/by Joie Warner.
    p.   cm.
Includes index.
ISBN 0-688-12704-5
1. Stir frying.   2. Wok cookery.   3. Skillet cookery
I. Title.
TX689.5.W37   1993
641.7′7 – dc20   93-14981
                                           CIP

Printed in the United States of America
First Edition
10 9 8 7 6 5 4 3 2 1

This book was created and produced by

Flavor Publications, Inc.
208 East 51st Street, Suite 240
New York, New York 10022

CONTENTS

INTRODUCTION

STIR-FRYING IS JUST right for the '90s: it stresses freshness and natural flavors, it's fast, it's fun, it's easy, it's economical, and, best of all, it's good for you. Although stir-frying is often identified with Chinese cooking, other recipes from other cuisines can be adapted to this remarkable cooking method. And although a wok is the ideal utensil for tossing ingredients easily and tidily, a large nonstick skillet is just as good – actually I often use a nonstick skillet for the simple reason that less oil is needed to prevent food from sticking. You may of course cook with virtually no oil in a nonstick pan if need be, but some oil is necessary to coat the ingredients to prevent scorching, help seal in flavor, and provide texture.

While stir-frying is one of the easiest techniques to master, there are a few secrets to its success: always cook bite-size pieces of food briskly over intense heat. The rapid cooking of vegetables over high heat ensures they retain their flavor and nutrients, stay brightly colored, crisp, and fragrant. As for meat, poultry, and fish, they remain tender and moist, too.

It is imperative to use the correct cooking vessel – a *heavy* iron wok or a large heavy nonstick skillet (see page 10). A large heavy cast-iron skillet is also an excellent choice as long as it has formed its own natural nonstick surface from many years of use. Enameled ware from France is also good, especially when cooking with acid foods like lemon or tomatoes.

Always read through the recipe before beginning, measuring and preparing all the ingredients ahead of time. It is important to cut each ingredient into more-or-less uniform pieces so that they all reach doneness at the same time. Set the ingredients – solid ingredients in separate piles, sauce in a small bowl – on a tray beside the stove ready to use in the proper sequence. Stir-frying proceeds swiftly – there is absolutely no time to stop to prepare the sauce or assemble and cut the ingredients.

To begin stir-frying, the wok (use a traditional bowl-shaped wok for gas stoves and a flat-bottomed wok for electric ranges) or skillet is placed over high heat and preheated for a minute or two or until you notice a small whiff of smoke on the surface of the pan. (Don't use the metal ring stand for stir-frying – it keeps the wok too far from the heat.) The oil is then added and allowed to heat for several seconds. (If using a nonstick pan, the oil is added first and heated until hot.) Now you must act quickly. If you allow the pan to heat up too much, the food will burn, but the heat must remain on high throughout the cooking process. Conversely, if the pan isn't hot enough, the ingredients will steam-cook, becoming soggy and ruining the dish. Once the oil is heated, the aromatic seasonings such as ginger and garlic are added and cooked for about three seconds or until fragrant. The meat and vegetables are added (they should sizzle) in the order in which the recipe specifies. Speed, dexterous tossing to keep the food moving, and timing are the essentials to success now as most ingredients take only seconds or a minute or two to cook. Use your senses – your eyes to detect when vegetables become brighter, indicating they are still crisp but tender – your nose to detect that peek-of-perfection aroma. The sauce is then restired to ensure the cornstarch is thoroughly combined – cornstarch tends to settle in the bottom – before pouring it into the pan to be stirred constantly until the sauce is thickened and smooth. Serve the dish at once to preserve the fresh taste and colors of the stir-fry. Last but not least, never add more ingredients than the recipe specifies: too much food in the pan will drastically lower the heat. This slows down the whole cooking process, causing the food to simmer and steam-cook, and to get overcooked before the heat can fully recover. If you must double a recipe, stir-fry the dish in two separate batches.

Stir-frying is one of best ways to create delicious, healthy meals in the shortest possible time. *All the Best Stir-Fries* is about the preparation of such meals. I've been eating and cooking Chinese food for many years and have developed quick and simple stir-fry recipes based on foods easily found in supermarkets and Asian food shops. Most of my recipes are inspired from dishes I've enjoyed in Chinatowns across America as well as recipes that I've adapted to the stir-fry method from other cuisines.

In the following chapters you'll find everything you need to know about stir-frying, as well as delicious recipes such as Thai Chicken Curry, Jasmine Rice, Italian Stir-Fried Chicken, Stir-Fried Sweet and Spicy Peanuts, Easy Mu Shu Pork, and Korean Noodles – plus notes on equipment and ingredients.

Now that Asian ingredients are no longer exotic – most are readily available in supermarkets and specialty stores – I hope to inspire you to begin tossing up tasty, tempting, no-fuss meals in a matter of minutes.

JOIE WARNER

NOTE: To use less oil in the following recipes, stir-fry in a nonstick skillet – not a wok which requires more oil – and lightly coat pan with nonstick cooking spray instead of the 1 to 2 tablespoons oil shown.

◆ ◆ ◆

BASICS

THE WOK

The Chinese wok is the world's most versatile cooking utensil – perfectly designed for every stove-top cooking method from stir-frying to deep-frying. The classic bowl-shaped wok – the one most cooks are familiar with – is perfect for use on a gas stove: the flames curl up around the wok providing the maximum, even heat essential for stir-frying. A variation on the classic design – the flat-bottomed wok – works best on electric stoves: it sits directly on the burner to get the highest heat possible. Woks come in a variety of sizes and materials – a 14– to 16-inch diameter wok is the most desirable size for home use. The best conductors of heat are the carbon-steel and cast-iron woks. Stainless steel, aluminum, electric, and nonstick-coated woks are poor conductors of heat and will never become hot enough for stir-frying. Don't use the ring stand accessory with a wok when stir-frying – it keeps the pan too far from the heat source. (The ring stand provides a secure base for deep-frying or steaming.) Another accessory – the wok lid – is used for combination stir-fry-steam-cooking of tougher vegetables such as broccoli.

CARING FOR YOUR WOK

New woks must be thoroughly cleaned of the rust-resistant coating, then "seasoned" before use. Thoroughly wash the wok in hot, soapy water several times, using a scouring pad. Rinse very well, completely dry the wok, then place it on high heat for a few minutes. Swirl in about 2 tablespoons vegetable oil, rotating the wok to coat it evenly. Toss in a few slices of ginger and whole garlic cloves and cook a few minutes, then discard. Clean the wok by wiping with paper towels and repeat 2 or 3 times using new oil and seasonings. Finally, wash the wok using a sponge or wok brush – never again a scouring pad – then rinse and dry thoroughly. Place the wok back over high heat for several seconds to ensure it's dry, rubbing a little vegetable oil over the surface to prevent rust. The wok will continue to darken with continued use, eventually creating its own natural nonstick coating. Store your wok in a well-ventilated area and use it often. Keeping a wok in an airless cupboard will cause the thin film of oil to turn rancid. Once your wok becomes "seasoned", it won't be necessary to rub a thin film of oil over the surface to prevent rust, but it must always be carefully dried. Never, ever scrub away the "seasoning" with a harsh scrubber or cleanser or put a wok in the dishwasher – a blackened wok is the pride of every first-rate stir-fry cook. To prevent acid foods from "eating away" the seasoning, I always use my large nonstick skillet to cook dishes which contain lemon juice and the like.

THE SKILLET

A large (12-inch) nonstick skillet is a superb substitute for a wok as long as it's of excellent quality – it should be heavy, not flimsy. The one advantage nonstick skillets have over woks is that less vegetable oil is needed. Woks must always be preheated over high heat before the vegetable oil is added to prevent foods from sticking. Not so the nonstick skillet: the oil is always added at the same time the pan is preheated – but the pan and oil must be hot before any ingredients are added.

Third and fourth options for stir-frying are a well-seasoned, large, heavy cast-iron skillet – or a large French enameled skillet – which also have good heating properties.

OTHER STIR-FRY EQUIPMENT

A wooden spatula or the Chinese-style metal spatula is necessary to properly toss the ingredients in a wok or skillet. I prefer a wooden spatula because it doesn't scratch the "seasoning" and it's not as noisy. (Always use a wooden spatula for nonstick surfaces.)

Another essential accessory is a Chinese cleaver or very sharp chef's knife. A cleaver is especially versatile – it not only chops the ingredients, but is very effective for scraping up and transporting chopped ingredients to your wok.

Chopsticks are ideal eating utensils, as well as excellent tools for mixing and for picking up and transferring ingredients during preparation.

CUTTING AND SLICING CHICKEN FOR STIR-FRYING

When cutting chicken breast meat for stir-frying, I've found that it's best cut into strips – about ¼ inches wide by 2 inches long – as opposed to cube-shaped pieces – in order to obtain the right textural quality. In most cases, it's chicken thigh meat that is cut into cube shapes – not white meat. If a recipe indicates thigh meat, do not substitute breast meat – and vice versa. The correct cutting of white and dark meat as well as using the type of meat specified in each recipe is very important to ensure tender, moist results.

TO BONE CHICKEN THIGHS

To bone chicken thighs, remove and discard skin. Stand the thigh upright and, using a sharp knife, cut around the top of the bone to sever meat and tendons. Make a vertical cut from top to bottom, then scrape the knife down the bone to separate the meat from the bone. Lay the meat out flat, remove any large tendons, and use the top, blunt edge of a cleaver or chef's knife to pound both sides in various directions to tenderize. Or ask your butcher to debone chicken thighs for you.

TEN SECRETS TO SUCCESSFUL STIR-FRYING

1. First and foremost, don't let the long list of ingredients in a stir-fry recipe intimidate you. A typical stir-fry has 3 or 4 parts: a main ingredient and its marinade; the seasonings (usually ginger and garlic); some vegetables, and the sauce ingredients. It's not as complicated as it appears at first sight.

2. Read the recipe through, then prepare and assemble the ingredients. Everything must be cut and marinated according to the recipe, the sauce mixed in advance, and all set in separate piles or bowls on a tray beside the wok before proceeding. Though I prefer cutting or chopping the aromatic seasonings and vegetables just prior to cooking to preserve vitamins and flavor, it can all be done ahead of time, covered, and refrigerated until ready to cook – but do bring everything back to room temperature before stir-frying.

3. Always preheat the wok or heavy skillet over high heat for a minute or two – until you detect a small whiff of smoke on the surface – before adding the oil. (If using a nonstick skillet, heat the oil and the skillet at the same time until very hot.)

4. Heat the oil for several seconds until hot but not smoking before adding the ingredients.

5. The heat must be kept at the maximum high temperature during the entire cooking process. If ingredients begin to burn, lift the wok off the element for a few seconds only – never turn the heat down. Don't worry, though, if ingredients become *lightly* charred – this adds that wonderful Chinatown flavor – what the Chinese call "wok hey" meaning wok fragrance.

6. Work quickly, adding ingredients in the sequence specified, tossing them fairly constantly to ensure that every surface is coated with oil and seared to seal in flavor and moisture. The term stir-frying and tossing are used interchangeably in my recipes – both meaning the continual stirring and gentle tossing (not like a salad!) of the ingredients. Vegetables are usually stir-fried first, starting with the toughest, and finishing with the tenderest, then removed to a plate. The meat or seafood is then added and once it's cooked, the vegetables are returned to the pan.

7. Never overload the wok or skillet. Don't add more ingredients than the recipe specifies or the pan will cool down, causing the food to steam-cook and become soggy or tough. If you are serving more guests than the recipe will provide for, simply prepare another dish or two. The general rule is to serve one dish for each person at the meal, e.g., four dishes (plus rice) for four persons, six dishes for six persons.

8. Use your senses. Your stove and equipment are not identical to mine so there will be slight variations to the cooking times I suggest in my recipes. Let your eyes and nose tell you when everything is cooked to perfection.

9. Always restir the sauce ingredients to recombine the cornstarch that inevitably settles to the bottom of the bowl – I leave a chopstick or spoon over the sauce bowl to remind me to do this – before adding it to the pan, then stir until the ingredients are lightly glazed.

10. When the dish is ready, serve it at once. Like a soufflé, a stir-fry waits for no one!

INGREDIENTS

BAMBOO SHOOTS: The edible, ivory-colored shoots of large bamboo plants, appreciated for their crunch and refreshing taste. For convenience, I prefer the canned ones which are available presliced into strips. Rinse them in cold water before using to remove the canned taste.

BEAN CURD: Fresh bean curd – or tofu – is made from soy beans that have been soaked, boiled, then pressed, and drained until the curd forms. It is high in protein, low-calorie, and has no cholesterol. Its bland flavor combines well with other foods. Bean curd is sold in plastic containers in the refrigerator section of Chinese grocery stores and supermarkets. Store in the refrigerator for about 1 week in cold water that is changed daily.

BEAN SPROUTS: These crisp and crunchy shoots are germinated from soy beans and, more commonly, mung beans. They are sold by weight in Chinese grocery stores and supermarkets. Choose only bright-white, absolutely crisp sprouts. Store them in a large bowl of cold water in the refrigerator for 3 to 4 days at most. Avoid canned beans sprouts.

BEAN THREAD NOODLES: Also known as cellophane and transparent noodles. These threadlike, dry white noodles are made from mung bean starch and become soft and gelatinous when soaked. I purchase a brand where several small cellophane packages (about 2 ounces each) are encased in pink plastic webbing.

CHICKEN BROTH: I use good-quality (low-salt) canned chicken broth – undiluted – in my stir-fry recipes and save my homemade stock for other uses such as homemade soups.

CHILI OIL: A hot oil made from an infusion of red chili peppers, garlic, and vegetable oil. Many brands are quite flavorless and mild, so it's best to sample a few until you find the one you like.

CHILI PASTE WITH SOY BEAN: Or substitute Garlic Paste with Chili. A hot, reddish-colored condiment made from chilies, garlic, soy beans, and salt. Don't substitute chili paste in recipes calling for Hot Bean Sauce and vice versa. Lan Chi brand from Taiwan is best.

CHINESE DRIED BLACK MUSHROOMS: These are woodsy, strong flavored dried shiitake mushrooms. I snap off the stems before soaking the caps in hot water. Sold in cellophane bags and clear plastic boxes in Chinese grocery stores, they last indefinitely in a covered container.

CORIANDER: Also called Chinese parsley and cilantro. It looks like flat parsley but has an unmistakable, pungent flavor and aroma that I love. Coriander can be found in Asian grocery stores and supermarkets. Choose bunches with bright green, unblemished leaves, preferably with roots attached. Store in refrigerator for 4 to 5 days submerged in a large bowl of cold water covered with plastic wrap.

DRY SHERRY: Buy a good medium-priced brand because a cheap sherry will impart an unpleasant taste. I prefer a lightly dry Spanish sherry called *El Cid* which blends well with Chinese ingredients.

GARLIC: I use fresh garlic in generous quantities in my cooking. When purchasing garlic, always look for firm, plump cloves.

GINGER: Fresh ginger is an essential ingredient in Chinese cooking. Choose ginger with shiny, smooth skin. Never substitute dry or powdered ginger.

HOISIN SAUCE: A thick, dark brown sauce made from soy beans, flour, sugar, vinegar, garlic, and chili, used as a flavoring, a dip, and a spread. Available in Chinese grocery stores and supermarkets. Keep in the refrigerator after opening. I recommend Koon Chun Sauce Factory brand (blue and yellow label), bottled (not canned).

HOT BEAN SAUCE: Also called Chili Bean Sauce, it is used as a hot and spicy condiment or seasoning. This sauce is available in Chinese grocery stores. Avoid brands containing salted black beans and check the label carefully to be sure the word "hot" or "chili" is on the label. Hot Bean Sauce is not a substitute for Chili Paste with Soy Bean and vice versa. My favorite brands are Har Har Pickle Food Factory (blue label) and Fu Chi brand.

OIL: I use canola oil, which has the same healthy qualities as olive oil. Peanut and corn oil are also very popular for stir-frying.

OYSTER SAUCE: A richly flavored sauce made from oyster extract, seasonings, and water, used to add flavor to sauces, meats, poultry, and vegetables. The best brands cost a little more, but are worth the extra expense. It keeps indefinitely in the refrigerator. My favorite brand is Hop Sing Lung.

RICE VINEGAR: Don't substitute regular white or cider vinegar in recipes calling for rice vinegar – they're too harsh. My favorite brands are Japanese, but check the label carefully and avoid any labeled "seasoned" rice vinegar. Rice vinegar is available in Asian grocery stores and some supermarkets.

SALTED BLACK BEANS: Also labeled Fermented Black Beans, they're made from fermented soy beans (turning them black), then dried, and salted. Pleasantly pungent, I never rinse them though some recipes suggest doing so. Packaged in plastic bags and cylindrical cardboard boxes, they are sold in Chinese grocery stores. Keep in a covered container in a dark, cool cupboard where they will keep for several years.

SESAME OIL: A fragrant and nutty oil made from roasted sesame seeds. I use a Japanese brand (Kadoya) rather than the Chinese brands which I've often found rancid tasting. Don't use the light-colored cold-pressed sesame oil found in health food stores – it doesn't have enough flavor. Store in refrigerator where it will last several months.

SOY SAUCE: Made from fermented soy beans, wheat, salt, and sugar, all the Chinese recipes in this book were created with Chinese soy sauce because Japanese brands (e.g., Kikkoman) impart a slightly sweeter flavor. You may substitute Japanese soy sauce if you wish, but avoid the synthetic brands available in many supermarkets. Pearl River Bridge Superior Soy Sauce is the brand I prefer.

STRAW MUSHROOMS (CANNED): So named because they are grown on beds of rice straw. Available in Asian grocers and some supermarkets.

SZECHUAN PEPPERCORNS: Also called flower pepper and wild pepper, these reddish-brown peppercorns aren't really peppers at all, but the dried berries of a shrub. They have a distinctive aroma, but aren't hot. They're sold in cellophane packages in Chinese grocery stores.

THAI COCONUT MILK: This liquid is obtained from pressing the coconut flesh, not the liquid found inside the coconut. I use the unsweetened canned coconut milk (not the sweetened coconut cream for drinks!). The best coconut milk comes from Thailand. Stir it well before using, the cream tends to rise to the top. The brand I use has a picture of a measuring cup and a coconut on the label. It's available in Asian food stores and some supermarkets.

THAI FISH SAUCE: The Thai name for this fermented fish sauce is *nam pla* (in Vietnam it's called *nuoc nam*). It is used as a condiment and seasoning ingredient in Southeast Asian cooking. A good quality fish sauce is Squid Brand from Thailand. It's available in Asian food shops and some supermarkets.

THAI RED CURRY PASTE: Available in Asian markets, red curry paste is a hot-and-spicy mixture of red chilies, garlic, ginger, coriander, turmeric, lemongrass and other seasonings. Curry powder is not a substitute for curry paste.

TREE EARS: Also called wood ears, cloud ears, and black fungus, this dried tree lichen is brown or black in color and used both medicinally and as a vegetable in stir-fries where it adds texture, rather than flavor. Rinse them thoroughly before soaking in hot water where they expand to 3 or 4 times their original size. Available in Chinese grocery stores in cellophane packages. They keep indefinitely at room temperature in a covered container.

◆ ◆ ◆

APPETIZERS

♦ ♦ ♦

Spring rolls are easy to make – if a little time consuming. Most cookbook authors would say "it's fun to get the whole family involved in the production," but in real life, I'm the one and only cook! But I don't mind: I just turn up the hi-fi and listen to some of my favorite old jazz classics and the work does seem to go faster. ◆ You must fry the rolls soon after they're stuffed, but you can stir-fry the filling up to a day in advance and keep it refrigerated (covered) before using.

SHRIMP AND VEGETABLE SPRING ROLLS

1 tablespoon soy sauce
2 teaspoons Japanese sesame oil
1 teaspoon salt
1 teaspoon sugar
½ teaspoon five spice powder
2 teaspoons cornstarch
3 tablespoons vegetable oil
2 large garlic cloves, chopped
2 tablespoons finely chopped fresh ginger
½ pound cooked small shrimp
½ pound Chinese barbecued pork, cut into ¼-inch thick strips
5 Chinese dried black mushrooms, soaked for 30 minutes in hot water, squeezed dry, caps thinly sliced
6 large whole green onions, finely chopped
1 large rib celery, finely chopped
1 large carrot, cut into fine julienne
1 pound fresh bean sprouts (not rinsed)
13-ounce package spring roll skins, thawed in package
1 large egg, beaten
3 cups vegetable oil
Worcestershire sauce for serving
Plum sauce for dipping

COMBINE SOY SAUCE, sesame oil, salt, sugar, five spice powder, and cornstarch in small bowl.

Heat oil in large nonstick skillet or preheated wok over high heat. When hot, add garlic, ginger, shrimp, pork, mushrooms, green onions, celery, and carrot and stir-fry for 2 minutes or until vegetables crisp-tender. Add bean sprouts; toss for 1 minute – no longer. Restir soy-sauce mixture, add to pan, and toss until combined. Immediately remove to a large baking sheet, spreading out mixture to allow it to cool quickly. Cool completely to room temperature before using.

Flex spring-roll package several times before opening. Open and carefully peel back one wrapper working from the outer edge to the middle, then peel off. Repeat and stack remaining wrappers. Cover with a damp cloth.

Put about 2 heaping tablespoons filling in center of lower half of wrapper; fold over from bottom fairly tightly to cover filling. Then roll to center. Fold the two sides toward center; moisten sides and top flap generously with beaten egg and continue rolling to form a cylinder. Make sure it is completely sealed. Set aside, seam side down. Repeat until all rolls are done. Cook within an hour of filling.

Heat oil in a preheated wok or deep-fryer to 375°F. Fry rolls in batches of 4 to 6 for 2 to 3 minutes or until golden brown, turning occasionally. Transfer rolls with tongs to drain on newspaper or brown paper grocery bag. Serve immediately with Worcestershire sauce and/or plum sauce. Makes about 24 rolls.

green
onion

Vietnamese and Thai spring rolls are made with rice paper – a translucent wrapper made from rice starch and water. These irresistible little bundles of transparent noodles and crunchy vegetables wrapped in rice paper are deep-fried, then dipped in a sweet and tangy sauce. ◆ The rolls can be prepared a day ahead, covered, and refrigerated, then fried at the last moment.

RICE PAPER SPRING ROLLS

¼ cup water
¼ cup rice vinegar
¼ cup sugar
1 to 2 tablespoons Thai fish sauce
1 teaspoon red pepper flakes
¼ cup shredded carrot
1 garlic clove, minced
½ teaspoon chili oil
4 ounces bean thread noodles, soaked for 10 minutes (no longer) in hot water and drained
1 tablespoon vegetable oil
2 garlic cloves, chopped
1 tablespoon finely chopped fresh ginger
2 large green onions (green part only), shredded

2 medium tree ears, soaked in hot water for 20 minutes, and thinly sliced (¼ cup)
2 medium carrots, shredded (½ cup)
2 tablespoons finely chopped fresh coriander
2 teaspoons sugar
½ teaspoon salt
About 36 triangular rice paper wrappers
2 cups vegetable oil
Boston lettuce leaves, thick stems removed, torn into 36 pieces about 5 x 3 inches
Fresh mint sprigs

COMBINE FIRST 8 INGREDIENTS in small serving bowl; set dipping sauce aside.

Using scissors, cut drained noodles into 1-inch pieces.

Heat oil in large nonstick skillet or preheated wok over high heat. When hot, add garlic, ginger, green onions, tree ears, carrots, and coriander; stir-fry for several seconds or until fragrant. Remove from heat and stir in noodles, sugar, and salt; set aside to cool.

Fill large bowl with warm water. Working with six at a time, lightly dampen each wrapper by quickly dipping in water; put them in single layer on clean dish towel and wait several seconds until softened. Place about 1 tablespoon filling in center of each wrapper, fold in sides over filling, then fold up bottom flap halfway, and roll over; press to seal.

Heat oil in wok or large skillet to 350°F and cook only 4 rolls at a time, taking care not to let them touch or they'll stick together. Cook for about 2 minutes or until golden; drain well on paper towels. Transfer to large lettuce-lined platter edged with mint sprigs. To eat, top a spring roll with 1 mint leaf, roll up in a lettuce leaf, and dip in sauce. Makes about 36 rolls.

coriander

E njoy these garlicky shrimp as
an appetizer served with
crusty bread, or as a main
course with fluffy white rice
(page 66) and a tossed green salad.
A squeeze of lime or lemon can be added
at the last moment, if desired.

SPANISH GARLIC SHRIMP

3 tablespoons olive oil	1 pound raw shrimp,
4 large garlic cloves, finely	peeled, deveined, and
chopped	patted dry
¼ teaspoon hot red pepper	½ teaspoon salt
flakes	2 tablespoons butter

HEAT OIL in large nonstick skillet or preheated wok over
high heat. When hot, add garlic, red pepper flakes, and
shrimp and stir-fry for 2 minutes or just until cooked
through. Sprinkle with salt and add butter, tossing several
seconds until butter is melted and hot. Serves 2 as a main
course with rice, 4 as an appetizer.

o tasty and addictive, bet you can't eat just one!

STIR-FRIED SWEET AND SPICY PEANUTS

2 teaspoons vegetable oil
1 teaspoon Japanese
    sesame oil
1 cup unsalted peanuts
¼ cup sugar

1 teaspoon salt
¼ teaspoon cayenne
1 teaspoon ground cumin
1 tablespoon sugar

HEAT BOTH OILS in medium nonstick skillet or preheated wok over medium-high heat. Add peanuts and stir to coat evenly with oil. Sprinkle with ¼ cup sugar, salt, cayenne, and cumin and stir-fry for 2 minutes or until sugar melts and beings to caramelize. Immediately remove from heat, sprinkle remaining sugar over peanuts and toss to coat evenly. Transfer peanuts to large piece of wax paper, spreading them in a single layer. Allow to cool before eating. Makes about 1 cup.

chicken

POULTRY

◆ ◆ ◆

ased on the Italian
specialty – veal piccata –
I replaced the veal with
chicken, fancied it up with
some green onion, pimentos, and red
pepper, and stir-fried the whole lot to
make a scrumptious dinner entrée. ◆
Pimentos – or pimientos – are available
in supermarkets, or specialty food stores
in glass jars, usually in the pickle section
next to the capers and the like. ◆ Serve
with rice and perhaps Italian Green Bean
and Mushroom Stir-Fry (page 89).

ITALIAN STIR-FRIED CHICKEN

¼ cup all-purpose flour
Salt
Freshly ground black
  pepper
2 skinless, boneless
  chicken breast halves
  (½ pound), cut into
  ¼-inch thick strips
1 tablespoon olive oil
1 tablespoon butter
1 large garlic clove,
  chopped
1 large whole green onion,
  chopped

¼ cup finely julienned
  sweet red pepper
2 tablespoons coarsely
  diced pimentos
1 tablespoon drained
  capers
¼ teaspoon dried basil
2 tablespoons fresh
  lemon juice
Salt
Freshly ground black
  pepper

COMBINE FLOUR, SALT, AND PEPPER on piece of wax paper. Coat chicken strips with seasoned flour, shaking off excess.

Heat oil and butter in large nonstick skillet or preheated wok over high heat. When hot, add chicken and stir-fry for 3 minutes or until cooked through; remove to plate.

Add garlic, green onion, red pepper, pimento, and capers and toss for 1 minute or until fragrant. Return chicken to pan, add basil, lemon juice, salt, and pepper and toss for several seconds or just until heated through. Serves 2 as a main course with rice, 4 with other dishes.

GINGER PLUM SAUCE CHICKEN

2 skinless, boneless
  chicken breast halves
  (½ pound), cut into
  ¼-inch thick strips
1 tablespoon water
1 tablespoon cornstarch
¼ teaspoon salt
3 tablespoons vegetable oil
2 tablespoons plum sauce

2 tablespoons water
1 teaspoon sugar
1 teaspoon soy sauce
1 tablespoon finely
  chopped fresh ginger
½ cup toasted pecan halves
1 large whole green onion,
  cut into 1-inch pieces

COMBINE CHICKEN with water in small bowl, thoroughly stir in cornstarch and salt, then 1 tablespoon oil; set aside to marinate for 30 minutes or up to 24 hours, covered, in refrigerator.

Combine plum sauce, water, sugar, and soy sauce in small bowl.

Heat remaining oil in large nonstick skillet or preheated wok over high heat. When hot, add chicken and stir-fry for 3 minutes or until opaque and cooked through. Add ginger and cook several seconds, then toss in pecans and green onion. Restir plum-sauce mixture, add to pan, and stir until lightly glazed. Serves 2 as a main course with rice, 4 with other dishes.

A recent creation of mine, this charming combination of chicken, fresh ginger, plum sauce, and pecans is remarkably simple to prepare – and decidedly delicious. ♦ Avoid domestically-produced plum sauce – the best brands are from Hong Kong – my favorite is Koon Chun Sauce Factory brand with a blue and yellow label. ♦ Toast the pecans in a small dry skillet until fragrant, being careful not to let them burn.

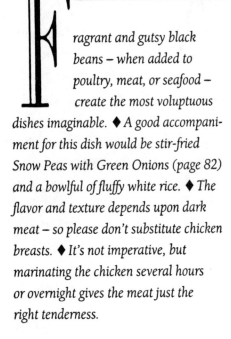

Fragrant and gutsy black beans – when added to poultry, meat, or seafood – create the most voluptuous dishes imaginable. ◆ A good accompaniment for this dish would be stir-fried Snow Peas with Green Onions (page 82) and a bowlful of fluffy white rice. ◆ The flavor and texture depends upon dark meat – so please don't substitute chicken breasts. ◆ It's not imperative, but marinating the chicken several hours or overnight gives the meat just the right tenderness.

CHICKEN WITH BLACK BEAN SAUCE

3 chicken thighs, skinned, boned (page 11) and cut into 1-inch cubes
1 tablespoon water
1 tablespoon cornstarch
¼ teaspoon salt
3 tablespoons vegetable oil
¼ cup chicken broth
2 teaspoons soy sauce
1 tablespoon oyster sauce
¼ teaspoon sugar
1 teaspoon cornstarch
1 medium-small onion, cut into wedges (8ths) and separated

½ medium sweet red pepper, seeded and cut into 1-inch pieces
2 large garlic cloves, chopped
1 tablespoon finely chopped fresh ginger
2 teaspoons salted black beans, chopped (not rinsed)

COMBINE CHICKEN with water in small bowl, thoroughly stir in cornstarch and salt, then 1 tablespoon oil; set aside to marinate for 30 minutes or up to 24 hours, covered, in refrigerator.

Combine chicken broth, soy sauce, oyster sauce, sugar, and cornstarch in small bowl.

Heat 1 tablespoon oil in large nonstick skillet or pre-heated wok over high heat. When hot, add onion and red pepper; stir-fry for 1 minute or until tender; remove to plate. Add garlic, ginger, and black beans and toss a few seconds or until fragrant. Add remaining oil, then chicken and stir-fry for 3 minutes or until opaque and cooked through. Return vegetables to pan; restir chicken-broth mixture and add, tossing several seconds or until lightly glazed. Serves 2 as a main course with rice, 4 with other dishes.

CHICKEN WITH TOASTED PECANS

2 skinless, boneless
  chicken breast halves
  (½ pound), cut into
  ¼-inch thick strips
1 tablespoon water
1 tablespoon cornstarch
¼ teaspoon salt
3 tablespoons vegetable oil
¼ cup chicken broth
1½ teaspoons soy sauce
1½ teaspoons dry sherry

1½ teaspoons
  Worcestershire sauce
1 tablespoon sugar
1½ teaspoons cornstarch
2 large garlic cloves,
  chopped
1 tablespoon finely
  chopped fresh ginger
3 large whole green onions,
  cut into 1-inch pieces
½ cup pecan halves, toasted

COMBINE CHICKEN with water in small bowl; thoroughly stir in cornstarch and salt, then 1 tablespoon oil; set aside to marinate for 30 minutes or up to 24 hours, covered, in refrigerator.

Combine chicken broth, soy sauce, sherry, Worcestershire sauce, sugar, and cornstarch in small bowl.

Heat 2 tablespoons oil in large nonstick skillet or preheated wok over high heat. When hot, add chicken and stir-fry for 3 minutes or until opaque and cooked through.

Add garlic, ginger, and green onions; stir-fry for 1 minute or until tender. Toss in pecans; restir chicken-broth mixture and add to pan, stirring until lightly glazed. Serves 2 as a main course with rice, 4 with other dishes.

H*ere's another popular China-town classic – with a twist. My rendering substitutes toasted pecans for standard cashew nuts – a stellar improvement, I think!* ◆ *My choice for the vegetable accompaniment: stir-fried spinach or watercress (and don't forget the rice!).* ◆ *Toast the nuts in an ungreased skillet until fragrant, being careful not to let them burn.*

Liver and onions are a classic combination. Here they're sweetened with a little honey and punctuated with plenty of ginger. Serve with white rice and a stir-fried vegetable. ◆ Don't overcook the livers or they'll be dry and tough.

CHICKEN LIVERS AND ONIONS WITH HONEY

1 pound chicken livers, trimmed and cut into 1-inch pieces
1 tablespoon soy sauce
1 tablespoon dry sherry
1 tablespoon cornstarch
2 tablespoons vegetable oil
1 medium-large onion, cut into wedges (8ths), and separated

1 generous tablespoon finely chopped fresh ginger
2 tablespoons soy sauce
2 tablespoons liquid honey
1/8 teaspoon salt

COMBINE CHICKEN LIVERS, soy sauce, and sherry in bowl; stir in cornstarch and transfer to fine-mesh footed strainer placed in sink. Gently shake strainer and let sit for 15 minutes to allow excess liquid to drain.

Heat 1 tablespoon oil in large nonstick skillet or preheated wok over high heat. Add onion and ginger and stir-fry for 1 minute or until tender; remove to plate. Add remaining oil and chicken livers; stir-fry for 2 minutes or until medium-rare. Return onions and ginger to pan; drizzle in soy sauce and honey, then sprinkle with salt. Toss for 1 minute or until glazed.Serves 2 to 4 as a main course with rice, 6 with other dishes.

CHICKEN WITH LIME ZEST, CHILES, AND BASIL

2 skinless, boneless
   chicken breast halves
   (½ pound), cut into
   ¼-inch thick strips
1 tablespoon water
1 tablespoon cornstarch
¼ teaspoon salt
2 tablespoons vegetable oil
2 large garlic cloves,
   chopped
Grated zest of 1 medium
   lime

2 whole green onions,
   shredded
2 fresh red chiles, seeded
   and cut into julienne
½ teaspoon sugar
1 tablespoon Thai
   fish sauce
¼ cup coarsely shredded
   fresh basil leaves

COMBINE CHICKEN with water in small bowl; thoroughly stir in cornstarch and salt, then 1 tablespoon oil; set aside to marinate for 30 minutes or up to 24 hours, covered, in refrigerator.

Heat 1 tablespoon oil in large nonstick skillet or pre-heated wok over high heat. When hot, add chicken and stir-fry for 3 minutes or until opaque and cooked through. Add garlic, lime zest, green onions, and chiles; toss for 1 minute or until tender. Add sugar, fish sauce, and basil and continue tossing for a few seconds more or until combined. Serves 2 as a main course with rice, 4 with other dishes.

I*'m just wild about this fiery hot, extraordinarily tasty, and very pretty chicken creation. ♦ Fresh red chiles and Thai fish sauce are available at Asian markets that carry ingredients from Thailand or Vietnam. ♦ Fish sauce, a seasoning liquid used mainly in Southeast Asia, has a fishy aroma that – quite surprisingly – adds the most wonderful flavor to many Far-Eastern dishes. ♦ The fresh chiles I use here are about 4- to 5-inches long and a little less than ½-inch thick – not the tiny, 1-inch, super-hot kind.*

Bursting with fresh flavor, this quick and simple stir-fry of rich-tasting Chinese barbecued duck, white crunchy bean sprouts, yellow egg ribbons, and green onions tastes as wonderful as it looks. ◆ Chinese barbecued duck is available in Chinese specialty stores – you see them glistening, festooned on hooks in the front window. I always buy a whole duck and use the leftovers – including the carcass – to make duck soup. The duck should be purchased only hours before serving and not refrigerated for best flavor – though it's not imperative. ◆ Whatever you do, don't overcook the sprouts – they should remain bright and crisp.

STIR-FRIED DUCK
WITH CRUNCHY VEGETABLES

1 teaspoon vegetable oil
2 eggs, well beaten
½ pound Chinese barbecued duck (2 duck breasts)
2 tablespoons vegetable oil
2 large garlic cloves, chopped
1 tablespoon finely chopped fresh ginger
3 large whole green onions, shredded
¾ pound very fresh bean sprouts (not rinsed)
2 tablespoons oyster sauce
½ teaspoon salt

HEAT 1 TEASPOON OIL in large nonstick skillet or preheated wok over high heat. When hot, add eggs; tilt pan to distribute egg into thin pancake and cook for 1 minute or just until set. Flip over and cook a few seconds to set other side. Transfer to cutting surface and cut into ¼-inch wide strips.

Remove and reserve skin from duck breasts, then cut away and discard layer of fat from skin. Thickly shred meat and skin.

Heat 2 tablespoons oil in large nonstick skillet or preheated wok over high heat. When hot, add garlic, ginger, and green onions; toss for 30 seconds. Add duck, egg strips, and bean sprouts; stir-fry for 30 seconds more or just until heated through. Add oyster sauce and sprinkle with salt. Toss until combined and serve at once. Serves 2 as a main course with rice, 4 with other dishes.

Sweet and Sour Chicken

3 skinless, boneless
   chicken breast halves
   (¾ pound), cut into
   1-inch cubes
1 extra-large egg, beaten
About ¾ cup cornstarch
⅓ cup sugar
⅓ cup ketchup
⅓ cup unsweetened
   pineapple juice

¼ cup cider vinegar
¼ cup vegetable oil
2 large garlic cloves,
   chopped
1 medium-small sweet red
   pepper, seeded and cut
   into 1-inch pieces
1 tablespoon cornstarch
   mixed with 1 tablespoon
   water

COMBINE CHICKEN and egg in bowl. Place cornstarch on large piece of wax paper; coat chicken cubes – one at a time – in cornstarch, then set them in single layer, not touching each other, on another large piece of wax paper.

Combine sugar, ketchup, pineapple juice, and vinegar in small bowl.

Heat oil in large nonstick skillet or preheated wok over high heat. When hot, add chicken and gently stir-fry for 3 minutes or until opaque and cooked through. Transfer chicken, with slotted spoon, to heatproof serving dish; keep warm in 250°F oven.

Remove all but 1 tablespoon oil; add garlic and red pepper and toss for 30 seconds or until crisp-tender. Stir in ketchup mixture; bring to a boil. Restir cornstarch mixture and pour into pan, stirring until sauce slightly thickens. Drizzle over chicken. Serves 2 as a main course with rice, 4 with other dishes.

Over the past several years, I've been visiting my local Chinatown restaurants to eat and carefully analyze my favorite dishes in order to discover the secrets to that true Chinatown flavor. The results of all my tasting and testing are the Asian recipes in this book, including this downright delicious sweet-and-sour dish. ◆ Pork tenderloin or any firm white fish such as sole, turbot, or halibut (¾ pound) may be substituted for the chicken.

S

weet, hot, and tart, this
fragrant sauce marries
extraordinarily well with
chicken, eggplant, and red
pepper strips. ◆ By the way, "fragrant
sauce" is simply a Szechuan mixture of
vinegar, sugar, and soy sauce that the
Chinese call "fish sauce" (not to be con-
fused with the Thai condiment named
fish sauce) because it is classically paired
with fish dishes.

CHICKEN IN FRAGRANT SAUCE

2 skinless, boneless
  chicken breast halves
  (½ pound), cut into
  ¼-inch thick strips
1 tablespoon water
1 tablespoon cornstarch
3 tablespoons vegetable oil
1 pound eggplant,
  unpeeled, stem removed,
  sliced into ½-inch thick
  strips
1½ teaspoons salt
¼ cup chicken broth
2 tablespoons sugar
2 tablespoons red wine
  vinegar

1 tablespoon soy sauce
1 teaspoon dry sherry
1 teaspoon Japanese
  sesame oil
1 sweet red pepper, seeded
  and sliced into thick
  julienne
2 large garlic cloves,
  chopped
1 tablespoon finely
  chopped fresh ginger
2 whole green onions,
  chopped
1 tablespoon hot bean
  sauce

COMBINE CHICKEN with water in small bowl, thoroughly
stir in cornstarch, then 1 tablespoon oil; set aside to
marinate for 30 minutes or up to 24 hours, covered, in
refrigerator.

Toss eggplant and salt in large colander; set in sink to
drain for 30 minutes. Pat dry with paper towels.

Combine chicken broth, sugar, vinegar, soy sauce, sherry,
and sesame oil in small bowl.

Heat 2 tablespoons oil in large nonstick skillet or preheated wok over high heat. When hot, add eggplant and
stir-fry for 3 minutes. Add red pepper and toss for 2 more
minutes or until tender; remove to plate.

Add chicken; stir-fry for 3 minutes or until cooked
through. Sprinkle with garlic, ginger, green onions, then stir
in bean sauce; toss for 1 minute. Return vegetables to pan,
restir chicken-broth mixture and add, tossing for 1 minute
to allow ingredients to absorb flavors. Serves 4 as a main
course with rice, 6 with other dishes.

LUSCIOUS LEMON CHICKEN

2 skinless, boneless chicken breast halves (½ pound), cut into 1-inch cubes
1 large egg, beaten
About ½ cup cornstarch
3 tablespoons sugar
3 tablespoons fresh lemon juice
¾ cup unsweetened pineapple juice
½ teaspoon Japanese sesame oil
¼ cup vegetable oil
2 large garlic cloves, chopped
1 tablespoon finely chopped fresh ginger
1 teaspoon salted black beans, coarsely chopped (not rinsed)
Grated zest of 1 medium lemon
2 teaspoons hot bean sauce
1 tablespoon cornstarch mixed with 1 tablespoon water
Grated lemon zest for garnish

COMBINE CHICKEN AND EGG in bowl. Place cornstarch on large piece of wax paper; coat chicken cubes – one at a time – in cornstarch, then set them in single layer, not touching each other, on another large piece of wax paper.

Combine sugar, lemon juice, pineapple juice, and sesame oil in small bowl.

Heat oil in large nonstick skillet or preheated wok over high heat. When hot, add chicken and gently stir-fry for 3 minutes or until cooked through. Transfer chicken, with slotted spoon, to heatproof serving dish; keep warm in 250°F oven.

Remove all but 1 tablespoon oil; add garlic, ginger, black beans, lemon zest, and bean sauce and toss for 30 seconds or until fragrant. Stir in lemon-juice mixture; bring to a boil. Restir cornstarch mixture and pour into pan, stirring until sauce slightly thickens. Drizzle over chicken and sprinkle with zest. Serves 2 as a main course with rice, 4 with other dishes.

D elightful and delicious, this stir-fry is a slight variation on a recipe from my book, A Taste of Chinatown. Always one to simplify a recipe whenever possible, I decided to stir-fry – instead of deep-fry – the chicken and was happy with the result. ♦ To show off this dish, serve it accompanied by Jasmine Rice (page 66) to soak up the utterly scrumptious sauce, and Hot and Spicy Green Beans (page 87) for contrast.

CHICKEN WITH CHINESE PICKLES

When I first tasted this unusual concoction in Chinatown, I figured you'd just have to be Chinese to be able to re-create it. (Though my Chinese friends have commented that – because of my passion for rice and genuine Chinese flavors and ingredients – I'm more Chinese than they are!) Well, happily I was wrong and I had no trouble devising this chicken and pickle alliance. ◆ In this recipe, I recommend stir-frying in a nonstick skillet – not a wok – otherwise the chicken sticks to the pan.

2 skinless, boneless chicken breast halves (½ pound), cut into ¼-inch thick strips
1 tablespoon water
1 tablespoon cornstarch
¼ teaspoon salt
2 tablespoons vegetable oil
3 tablespoons chicken broth
1 tablespoon dry sherry
1 teaspoon cornstarch
1 teaspoon Japanese sesame oil
¼ cup Ma Ling brand Pickled Cabbage, drained
½ cup matchstick-size shreds bamboo shoots
7 small Chinese dried black mushrooms, soaked 30 minutes in hot water, squeezed dry, caps thinly sliced
1 teaspoon sugar combined with 1 tablespoon vegetable oil
1 large garlic clove, chopped
1 tablespoon finely chopped fresh ginger

COMBINE CHICKEN with water in small bowl; thoroughly stir in cornstarch and salt, then 1 tablespoon oil; set aside to marinate for 30 minutes or up to 24 hours, covered, in refrigerator.

Combine chicken broth, sherry, cornstarch, and sesame oil in small bowl.

Heat ungreased large nonstick skillet over high heat. When hot, add pickled cabbage, bamboo shoots, and mushrooms and stir-fry for 30 seconds to remove excess moisture. Restir sugar-oil mixture; add to wok and toss for 30 seconds and remove to plate.

Add 1 tablespoon oil to pan; when hot, add chicken, garlic, and ginger and stir-fry for 3 minutes or until opaque and cooked through. Return pickle mixture to pan, restir chicken-broth mixture and add, stirring until lightly glazed. Serves 2 as a main course with rice, 4 with other dishes.

SPICY ORANGE CHICKEN WITH SNOW PEAS AND RED PEPPER

2 skinless, boneless
  chicken breast halves
  (½ pound), cut into
  ¼-inch thick strips
1 tablespoon water
1 tablespoon cornstarch
¼ teaspoon salt
3 tablespoons vegetable oil
¼ cup fresh orange juice
Finely grated zest of
  ½ medium orange
2 teaspoons sugar
2 teaspoons rice vinegar
1 teaspoon mushroom
  soy sauce

1 teaspoon chili paste with
  soy bean
1½ teaspoons cornstarch
¼ teaspoon Japanese
  sesame oil
1 large garlic clove,
  chopped
1 tablespoon finely
  chopped fresh ginger
½ small sweet red pepper,
  seeded and cut into
  julienne
10 large snow peas,
  trimmed and sliced
  in half lengthwise

COMBINE CHICKEN with water in small bowl; thoroughly stir in cornstarch and salt, then 1 tablespoon oil; set aside to marinate for 30 minutes or up to 24 hours, covered, in refrigerator.

Combine orange juice, orange zest, sugar, rice vinegar, mushroom soy sauce, chili paste, cornstarch, and sesame oil in small bowl.

Heat 1 tablespoon oil in large nonstick skillet or preheated wok over high heat. When hot, add garlic, ginger, red pepper, and snow peas and toss for 1 minute or until crisp-tender; remove to plate. Add 1 tablespoon oil, add chicken, and stir-fry for 3 minutes or until opaque and cooked through. Return vegetables to pan, restir orange-juice mixture and add, stirring until lightly glazed. Serves 2 as a main course with rice, 4 with other dishes.

A piquant, aromatic chicken toss with crunchy, bright-colored vegetables. ◆ Be sure the pan is hot before adding the vegetables in order to produce what the Chinese call "wok hey" or wok flavor – a few charred spots on the vegetables. ◆ Mushroom soy sauce is simply soy sauce flavored with mushrooms.

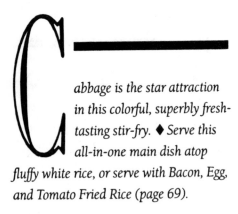

Cabbage is the star attraction in this colorful, superbly fresh-tasting stir-fry. ◆ Serve this all-in-one main dish atop fluffy white rice, or serve with Bacon, Egg, and Tomato Fried Rice (page 69).

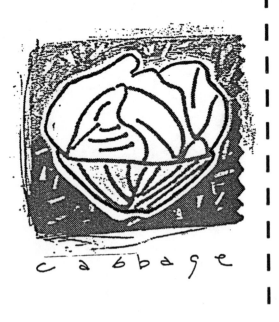

cabbage

CHICKEN WITH CABBAGE, RED PEPPER, AND GREEN BEANS

2 skinless, boneless
  chicken breast halves
  (½ pound), cut into
  ¼-inch thick strips
1 tablespoon water
1 tablespoon cornstarch
¼ teaspoon salt
3 tablespoons vegetable oil
½ cup chicken broth
1 tablespoon dry sherry
2 tablespoons oyster sauce
1 teaspoon Japanese
  sesame oil
¼ teaspoon sugar

1 tablespoon cornstarch
2 ounces green beans,
  trimmed and sliced in
  half lengthwise
1 large garlic clove,
  chopped
¼ pound green cabbage,
  cut into 1-inch wide
  strips
½ small sweet red pepper,
  seeded and cut into
  julienne
3 large whole green onions,
  shredded

COMBINE CHICKEN with water in small bowl, thoroughly stir in cornstarch and salt, then 1 tablespoon oil; set aside to marinate for 30 minutes or up to 24 hours, covered, in refrigerator.

Combine chicken broth, sherry, oyster sauce, sesame oil, sugar, and cornstarch in small bowl.

Heat 2 tablespoons oil in large nonstick skillet or pre-heated wok over high heat. When hot, add green beans; toss for 1 minute. Add garlic, cabbage, red pepper, and green onions and stir-fry for another minute or until crisp-tender; remove to plate. Add chicken and stir-fry for 3 minutes or until opaque and cooked through. Return vegetables to pan, restir chicken-broth mixture and add, tossing until sauce slightly thickens. Serves 2 as a main course with rice, 4 with other dishes.

THAI CHICKEN CURRY

2 tablespoons vegetable oil
¼ cup chopped red onion
1 large garlic clove, chopped
Grated zest of 1 medium-large lime
1 generous tablespoon Thai red curry paste
1 tablespoon best-quality curry powder
½ teaspoon hot red pepper flakes

6 chicken thighs, skinned, boned (page 11) and cut into 1-inch cubes
14-ounce can Thai coconut milk
1 tablespoon Thai fish sauce
1 teaspoon brown sugar
½ cup fresh basil leaves, shredded

HEAT OIL in large nonstick skillet or preheated wok over high heat. When hot, add onion, garlic, lime zest, curry paste, curry powder, and red pepper flakes. Cook, stirring, for 1 minute or until aromatic. Add chicken and stir-fry for 3 minutes or until opaque. Stir in coconut milk, fish sauce, and brown sugar. Reduce heat and simmer for 7 minutes or until chicken is tender and cooked through. Just before serving, sprinkle with basil. Serves 2 as a main course with rice, 4 with other dishes.

Thai curry paste, coconut milk, and fresh basil leaves infuse this hot and spicy chicken dish with intoxicating aromas and flavors. ◆ The Thai's love plenty of sauce to pour over rice, so don't be tempted to add more chicken. ◆ Naturally, fragrant Jasmine Rice (page 66) and Green Beans with Oyster Sauce (page 88) round out the meal perfectly. ◆ Don't even think of substituting chicken breasts for chicken thighs!

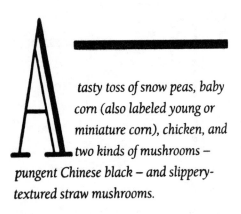

tasty toss of snow peas, baby corn (also labeled young or miniature corn), chicken, and two kinds of mushrooms – pungent Chinese black – and slippery-textured straw mushrooms.

CHICKEN WITH SNOW PEAS, BABY CORN, AND MUSHROOMS

2 skinless, boneless chicken breast halves (½ pound), cut into ¼-inch thick strips
1 tablespoon water
1 tablespoon cornstarch
¼ teaspoon salt
3 tablespoons vegetable oil
½ cup water
2½ tablespoons oyster sauce
¼ teaspoon sugar
1 teaspoon Japanese sesame oil

1 tablespoon cornstarch
2 large garlic cloves, chopped
16 snow peas, trimmed
16 canned whole baby corn, drained
12 canned straw mushrooms, drained and cut in half if large
6 small Chinese dried black mushrooms, soaked for 30 minutes in hot water, squeezed dry, caps thinly sliced

COMBINE CHICKEN with water in small bowl, thoroughly stir in cornstarch and salt, then 1 tablespoon oil; set aside to marinate for 30 minutes or up to 24 hours, covered, in refrigerator.

Combine water, oyster sauce, sugar, sesame oil, and cornstarch in small bowl.

Heat 1 tablespoon oil in large nonstick skillet or preheated wok over high heat. When hot, add garlic, snow peas, baby corn, and the two mushrooms and stir-fry for 1 minute or until heated through; remove to plate. Add remaining oil, then chicken and stir-fry for 3 minutes or until opaque and cooked through. Return vegetables to pan, restir oyster-sauce mixture and add, stirring until sauce slightly thickens. Serves 2 as a main course with rice, 4 with other dishes.

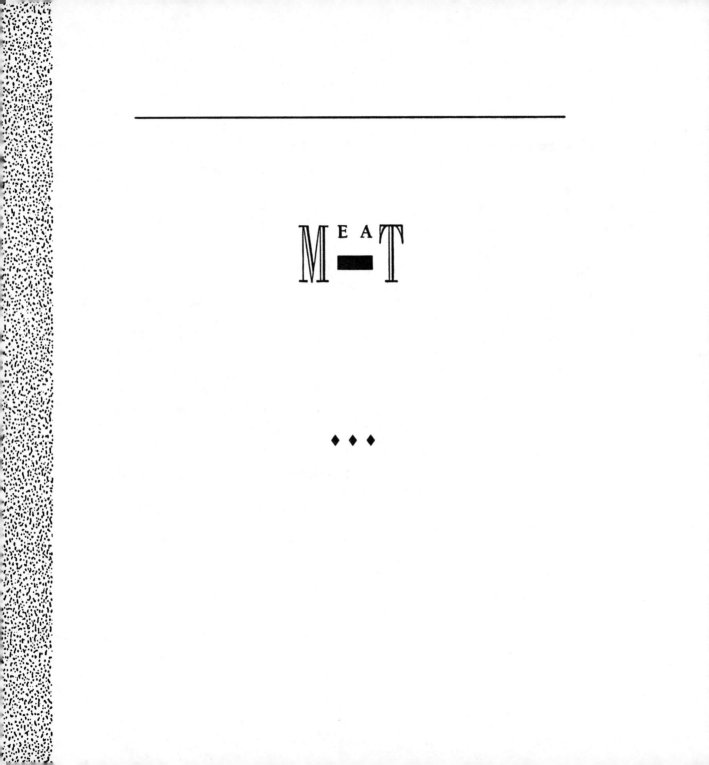

MEAT

♦ ♦ ♦

Another lively Thai specialty.
♦ Serve it atop Jasmine Rice
(page 66). ♦ If you always
have a bottle of soy sauce in
your pantry, I hope you'll add Thai fish
sauce, too. Don't shy away from its potent
aroma, it will impart a delicate, yet
toothsome flavor to many an Asian repast.

SPICY GROUND BEEF WITH BASIL

3 tablespoons vegetable oil
1 pound ground beef
½ teaspoon hot red pepper
  flakes
2 large garlic cloves,
  chopped

1½ tablespoons Thai fish
  sauce
1½ tablespoons soy sauce
1 cup fresh basil leaves,
  coarsely shredded

HEAT 2 TABLESPOONS OIL in large nonstick skillet or
preheated wok over high heat. When hot, add ground beef
and toss, breaking up meat with wooden spatula, until no
pink remains. Transfer to colander in sink and allow excess
oil to drain.

Add 1 tablespoon oil to skillet; when hot, add red pepper
flakes and garlic and cook for 1 minute. Return beef to pan;
add fish sauce and soy sauce and toss to combine. Stir-fry
for 30 seconds to allow ground beef to absorb flavors, then
stir in basil until combined. Serves 2 as a main course with
rice, 4 with other dishes.

GINGER BEEF

½ pound boneless top
sirloin, trimmed and
thinly sliced across the
grain into 2-inch long
strips
1 tablespoon soy sauce
2 teaspoons sugar
1 tablespoon finely
chopped fresh ginger
1 tablespoon cornstarch
3 tablespoons vegetable oil
1½ tablespoons soy sauce
1 tablespoon water
1 teaspoon sugar
1 teaspoon red wine
vinegar

1 teaspoon chili paste with
soy bean
½ teaspoon Japanese
sesame oil
¾ teaspoon cornstarch
1 large rib celery, leaves
removed and cut into
julienne
2 medium carrots, cut into
julienne
1 tablespoon water
2 large garlic cloves,
chopped
1 tablespoon finely
chopped fresh ginger
1 large whole green onion,
shredded

G

inger – with its clean, bracing flavor – is the perfect counterpoint to rich-tasting beef.

COMBINE BEEF with soy sauce, sugar, and ginger in small bowl. Thoroughly stir in cornstarch, then 1 tablespoon oil; set aside to marinate for 30 minutes or preferably 24 hours, covered, in refrigerator.

Combine soy sauce, water, sugar, vinegar, chili paste, sesame oil, and cornstarch in small bowl.

Heat 1 tablespoon oil in large nonstick skillet or pre-heated wok over high heat. When hot, add celery and carrots and stir-fry for 1 minute, then add 1 tablespoon water, cover, and cook for another minute or until tender; remove to plate.

Add 1 tablespoon oil, then beef and toss for 1 minute or until medium-rare. Sprinkle with garlic, ginger, and green onion; stir-fry 1 minute. Return vegetables to pan; restir soy-sauce mixture and add, stirring until sauce slightly thickens. Serves 2 as a main course with rice, 4 with other dishes.

SPICY SESAME BEEF STIR-FRY

S esame seeds lend their distinctive texture and nutty character to this tasty, colorful beef and vegetable stir-fry. ◆ The green beans can be blanched, chilled, and drained, then covered and refrigerated several hours ahead. Bring back to room temperature before proceeding.

½ pound boneless top sirloin, trimmed and thinly sliced across the grain into 2-inch long strips
1 tablespoon soy sauce
2 teaspoons sugar
1 tablespoon cornstarch
2 tablespoons lightly toasted sesame seeds plus extra for garnish
1 tablespoon chili oil
½ pound green beans, trimmed
6 tablespoons chicken broth

1 tablespoon soy sauce
1 tablespoon dry sherry
2 tablespoons oyster sauce
2 teaspoons cornstarch
½ teaspoon sugar
2 tablespoons vegetable oil
½ large sweet red pepper, seeded and cut into julienne
1 large garlic clove, chopped
1 tablespoon finely chopped fresh ginger

COMBINE BEEF with soy sauce, sugar, cornstarch, sesame seeds, and chili oil in small bowl.

Blanch beans in boiling water for 4 minutes or until tender but still bright green; plunge beans into ice water to chill, then drain. Pat dry with paper towels and cut in half lengthwise.

Combine chicken broth, soy sauce, sherry, oyster sauce, cornstarch, and sugar in small bowl.

Heat 1 tablespoon oil in large nonstick skillet or pre-heated wok over high heat. When hot, add green beans and red pepper and stir-fry for 1 minute; remove to plate.

Add 1 tablespoon oil, then beef and toss for 1 minute or until medium-rare. Sprinkle with garlic and ginger and stir-fry for 1 minute. Return vegetables to pan; restir chicken-broth mixture and add, stirring until sauce slightly thickens. Serves 2 as a main course with rice, 4 with other dishes.

CURRIED BEEF WITH TOMATOES

½ pound boneless top sirloin, trimmed and thinly sliced across the grain into 2-inch long strips
1 tablespoon soy sauce
½ teaspoon sugar
1 tablespoon cornstarch
2½ tablespoons vegetable oil
½ cup water
1 tablespoon cornstarch
1 tablespoon soy sauce
1 tablespoon Worcestershire sauce

3 tablespoons ketchup
1 teaspoon best-quality curry powder
2 strips bacon, diced
1 medium onion, cut into wedges (8ths) and separated
2 large garlic cloves, chopped
1 tablespoon finely chopped fresh ginger
2 ripe, medium tomatoes, cut into wedges (8ths)

COMBINE BEEF with soy sauce and sugar in small bowl. Thoroughly stir in cornstarch, then 1 tablespoon oil; set aside to marinate for 30 minutes or preferably 24 hours, covered, in refrigerator.

Combine water, cornstarch, soy sauce, Worcestershire sauce, ketchup, and curry powder in small bowl.

Cook bacon until crisp in large nonstick skillet or preheated wok over high heat; remove to plate leaving bacon fat in pan. Add about 2 teaspoons oil – if necessary – then onion and stir-fry for 1 minute or until tender; remove to plate with bacon.

Add 1 tablespoon oil – if necessary – and beef and toss for 1 minute or until medium-rare. Sprinkle with garlic and ginger and stir-fry for 30 seconds. Add tomatoes; toss for another 30 seconds or until heated through. Return onion and bacon to pan; restir soy-sauce mixture and add, stirring until sauce slightly thickens. Serves 3 as a main course with rice, 5 with other dishes.

When my Chinatown cookbook was published a few years ago, I received some letters from readers saying they wished I'd created a recipe for a favorite Cantonese specialty – slices of beef stir-fried with fresh tomatoes in a curry-flavored sauce. I played around with the ingredients several times before I came up with this interpretation. ◆ Fresh, ripe, flavorful tomatoes are a must.

I n Korea, marinated beef, called *bulgogi*, is cooked on a special cooker called a Genghis Khan grill, but I've adapted it to a stir-fry. ◆ *Serve with* *kim chee* *(Korean preserved vegetables)* *and rice, of course.* ◆ *It is important to cook the beef in three batches in a very hot pan: overloading the pan will cool it down, causing the beef to steam instead of brown.*

KOREAN SESAME BEEF

1 pound boneless top sirloin, trimmed and thinly sliced across the grain into 2-inch long strips
2 tablespoons soy sauce
2 teaspoons Japanese sesame oil
½ teaspoon sugar
1 large garlic clove, finely chopped
1 large green onion (green part only), chopped
¼ teaspoon freshly ground black pepper
2 tablespoons vegetable oil

COMBINE BEEF with soy sauce, sesame oil, sugar, garlic, green onion, and pepper in bowl; cover and refrigerate for several hours or overnight in refrigerator.

Heat 1 tablespoon oil in large nonstick skillet or pre-heated wok over high heat. When hot, add ⅓ of the beef and toss for 1 minute or until medium-rare; remove to plate and keep warm. Repeat twice more, adding more oil if necessary. Serve immediately. Serves 3 as a main course with rice, 4 with other dishes.

HOT ORANGE BEEF

½ pound boneless top sirloin, trimmed and thinly sliced across the grain into 2-inch long strips
1 tablespoon soy sauce
1 tablespoon sugar
1 tablespoon cornstarch
3 tablespoons vegetable oil
1 tablespoon water
2 teaspoons soy sauce
2 teaspoons red wine vinegar

2 teaspoons sugar
½ teaspoon cornstarch
½ teaspoon Japanese sesame oil
1 medium onion, cut into wedges (8ths) and separated
2 large garlic cloves, chopped
1 tablespoon grated orange zest
1 teaspoon hot red pepper flakes

COMBINE BEEF with soy sauce and sugar in small bowl. Thoroughly stir in cornstarch, then 1 tablespoon oil; set aside to marinate for 30 minutes or preferably 24 hours, covered, in refrigerator.

Combine water, soy sauce, red wine vinegar, sugar, cornstarch, and sesame oil in small bowl.

Heat 1 tablespoon oil in large nonstick skillet or preheated wok over high heat. When hot, add onion and stir-fry for 1 minute or until tender; remove to plate. Add remaining oil and beef and toss for 1 minute or until medium-rare. Return onion to pan, sprinkle with garlic, orange zest, and red pepper flakes; stir-fry for 1 minute. Restir soy-sauce mixture and add, stirring until lightly glazed. Serves 2 as a main course with rice, 4 with other dishes.

oth sweet and hot, this full-of-flavor beef stir-fry is supposed to be wickedly hot. My recipe is fairly fiery – but add more pepper flakes if you wish it truly torrid. ♦ The longer the beef marinates – preferably overnight – the tenderer it will be.

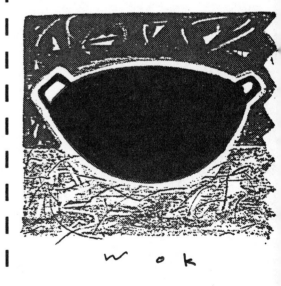

wok

S weet-tasting, hoisin-sauced pork shreds are traditionally served in Chinese pancakes. As these are time-consuming to prepare, I've substituted Mexican flour tortillas for a faster, no-fuss version.

HOISIN PORK SHREDS IN TORTILLA PANCAKES

¾ pound pork tenderloin, trimmed and cut into ¼-inch thick strips
2 teaspoons soy sauce
1 teaspoon dry sherry
¼ teaspoon Japanese sesame oil
1 teaspoon cornstarch
4 large whole green onions, shredded
2 tablespoons hoisin sauce

2 teaspoons sugar
2 teaspoons dry sherry
2 teaspoons soy sauce
2 tablespoons vegetable oil
½ cup matchstick-size shreds bamboo shoots
6 flour tortillas, wrapped completely in foil, warmed in 300°F oven for 10 minutes

COMBINE PORK with soy sauce, sherry, sesame oil, and cornstarch in small bowl; set aside to marinate while preparing other ingredients or leave, covered, overnight in refrigerator.

Just before beginning to cook, arrange green onion shreds attractively on serving dish.

Combine hoisin sauce, sugar, sherry and soy sauce in small bowl.

Heat oil in large nonstick skillet or preheated wok over high heat. When hot, add pork and stir-fry for 3 minutes or until cooked through. Restir hoisin-sauce mixture, add to pan, and toss for several seconds to glaze. Stir in bamboo shoots and immediately transfer to green-onion-lined dish. To eat, place some pork mixture and green onion in a warmed tortilla, fold it over and eat sandwich-style. Serves 3 as a main course with rice, 6 with other dishes.

Spicy Ground Pork

1 tablespoon vegetable oil
2 large garlic cloves, chopped
1 small onion, chopped
½ pound ground pork
1 tablespoon Thai red curry paste
1 teaspoon best-quality curry powder
1 tablespoon Thai fish sauce
¼ cup Thai coconut milk
1 teaspoon sugar
Grated zest of 1 medium lime

About 1 cup sliced unpeeled English cucumber
2 generous tablespoons coarsely chopped fresh basil leaves
2 generous tablespoons coarsely chopped fresh mint leaves
1 small green onion (green part only) chopped
2 tablespoons coarsely crushed toasted peanuts

HEAT OIL in large nonstick skillet or preheated wok over high heat. When hot, add garlic and onion and cook for 1 minute or until tender. Add pork and cook, breaking up meat with wooden spatula, until no pink remains. Stir in curry paste, curry powder, fish sauce, coconut milk, and sugar and cook for 2 minutes or until thickened. Sprinkle with lime zest, stir, and transfer to a small platter or serving dish edged with cucumber slices. Sprinkle with basil, mint, green onion, and peanuts. Serves 2 as a main course with rice, 4 with other dishes.

Ordinary ground pork is transformed into fabulous fare with just a few zesty Thai ingredients. ◆ As with almost every Asian stir-fry, the perfect accompaniment is white rice, and preferably another dish or two of complementary flavors. ◆ I place the peanuts in a plastic sandwich bag and use a rolling pin to coarsely crush them. ◆ Toast the peanuts in an small ungreased skillet until fragrant, being careful not to let them burn. ◆ This dish is _very_ hot and spicy.

Cooking pork twice – first simmered in water until very tender, then stir-fried in a sweet, slightly hot sauce – creates an incredibly rich, tender, and succulent dish of Szechuan origin. ◆ You will have more pork than you need for this recipe so you can perform an encore; or the leftover pork can be sliced paper thin for sandwiches, or added to Chinese soups. ◆ The cooked pork must be refrigerated several hours or overnight before stir-frying, so plan accordingly. ◆ Note that this dish is not cooked in a wok.

TWICE COOKED PORK

3 pounds boneless pork
  shoulder or butt
1 tablespoon dry sherry
1 tablespoon hot bean
  sauce
1 tablespoon hoisin sauce

1 tablespoon soy sauce
1 teaspoon sugar
2 tablespoons vegetable oil
1 large garlic clove,
  chopped

PLACE PORK in large saucepan with enough water to barely cover. Bring to a boil over high heat; reduce heat to medium-low, cover, and simmer for 2 hours or until meat is cooked through and very tender (poke a chopstick through the meat – if it goes through fairly easily it's ready). Remove meat from pot (reserving stock for soup if desired), cover, and refrigerate several hours or overnight to firm up the meat.

Cut pork into very thin slices about 2 x 2 inches with some of the fat attached – the fatty part is considered a delicacy. You will need 1 pound pork; reserve remaining pork for another use.

Combine sherry, hot bean sauce, hoisin sauce, soy sauce, and sugar in small bowl.

Heat oil in large nonstick skillet over high heat; add garlic and cook for several seconds. Add pork in single layer and cook for 1 minute or until heated through and fat becomes transparent. Turn with tongs and cook several seconds more or until heated through.

Restir sherry mixture, add to skillet, and gently stir-fry until pork slices are evenly coated. Serves 3 as a main course with rice, 5 with other dishes.

SPARERIBS WITH BLACK BEANS

2 tablespoons vegetable oil
1½ pounds meaty pork
    spareribs, cut into
    1½-inch pieces and any
    bone splinters removed
3 large garlic cloves, finely
    chopped
1 tablespoon finely
    chopped fresh ginger
1 tablespoon salted black
    beans, coarsely chopped
    (not rinsed)

1 cup chicken broth
1 tablespoon soy sauce
1 tablespoon dry sherry
1 teaspoon sugar
¼ teaspoon salt
1 tablespoon cornstarch
    mixed with 1 tablespoon
    water

HEAT OIL in large nonstick skillet or preheated wok over medium-high heat. When hot, add ribs and toss for 2 minutes or until browned. Add garlic, ginger, and black beans and stir-fry for several seconds or until fragrant. Add chicken broth, soy sauce, sherry, sugar, and salt and bring to a boil. Reduce heat to medium-low, cover, and simmer for 1 hour or until tender, stirring occasionally. Remove cover; turn heat to high, restir cornstarch mixture, and drizzle into wok, stirring until sauce slightly thickens. Serves 4 as a main course with rice, 6 with other dishes.

E*arthy Chinese black beans give these bite-size ribs extra punch. ♦ If you don't have a heavy cleaver and a mallet, have your butcher cut the spareribs for you. ♦ There's plenty of sauce to pour over rice, or you can add another ½ pound ribs if you like. ♦ Serve the ribs with rice accompanied by a stir-fried vegetable.*

Not even my Chinese friends notice when I cheat and use readily available Mexican flour tortillas in place of homemade Mandarin pancakes! ◆ Mu Shu Pork – for those who have never partaken of this enormously popular Chinese dish – is a deliciously sweet and savory mixture of pork and vegetables wrapped in Chinese "pancakes".

EASY MU SHU PORK

½ pound pork tenderloin, trimmed and cut into ¼-inch thick strips
2 teaspoons soy sauce
½ teaspoon dry sherry
¼ teaspoon sugar
⅛ teaspoon salt
½ teaspoon cornstarch
10 (6-inch) flour tortillas
2½ tablespoons vegetable oil
2 eggs, well beaten with ¼ teaspoon salt
1½ ounces bean thread noodles, soaked in hot water for 10 minutes (no longer) and drained
2 tablespoons soy sauce
2 tablespoons dry sherry

1 tablespoon Japanese sesame oil
½ teaspoon sugar
1 large tree ear, soaked in hot water 20 minutes, knobby part cut off, and thinly sliced (½ cup)
4 medium Chinese dried black mushrooms, soaked for 30 minutes in hot water, squeezed dry, caps thinly sliced
3 whole green onions, shredded
½ cup julienned sweet red pepper
½ cup matchstick-size shreds bamboo shoots
Hoisin sauce for serving

COMBINE PORK with next five ingredients; set aside. Wrap tortillas in foil and place in 350°F oven to warm for 10 minutes.

Heat 1½ teaspoons oil in large nonstick skillet or pre-heated wok over high heat. Add eggs, tilting pan to dis-tribute into thin pancake and cook just until set. Transfer to cutting surface and cut into ¼-inch wide strips. Cut bean threads with scissors into 2-inch pieces. Combine soy sauce, sherry, sesame oil, and sugar in small bowl.

Heat 2 tablespoons oil in large nonstick skillet or pre-heated wok over high heat. When hot, add pork; stir-fry for 2 minutes or until no longer pink. Add tree ear, mush-rooms, green onions, red pepper, and bamboo shoots; toss a few seconds, then add bean thread noodles and egg strips. Restir soy-sauce mixture and add, tossing until combined. Transfer to platter and serve with warmed tortillas. To eat, spread a little hoisin sauce over tortilla, place some pork mixture on top, fold it over and eat sandwich-style. Serves 4 as a main course, 8 with other dishes.

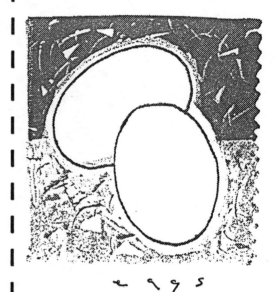

eggs

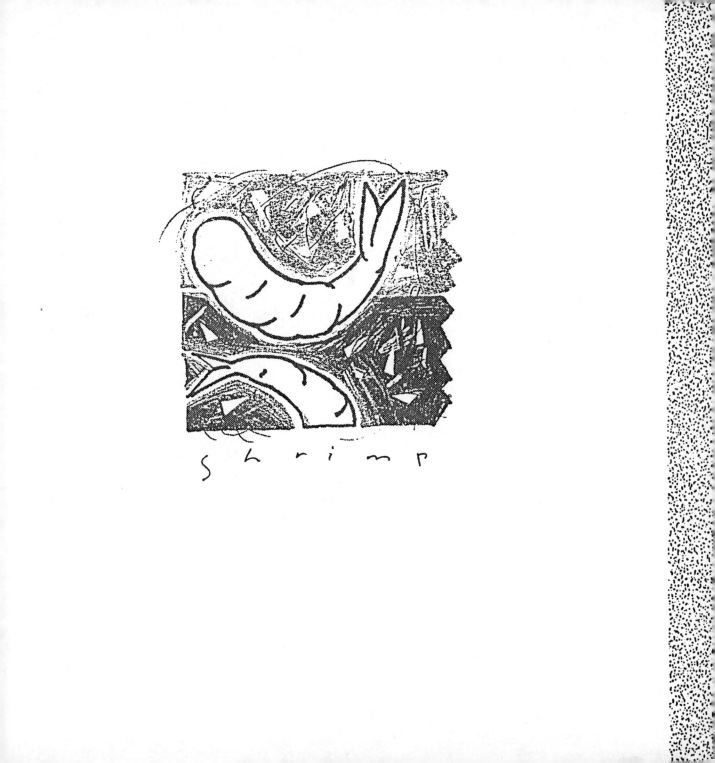

shrimp

SEAFOOD

♦ ♦ ♦

hen making the dip, you need to "cook" the vegetable and chili oils, otherwise the dip will taste oily.

HONG KONG SHRIMP

3 tablespoons soy sauce
1 teaspoon rice vinegar
1 green onion (green part only) finely chopped
1 tablespoon vegetable oil
1 tablespoon chili oil

¾ pound raw shrimp, peeled and deveined
1 teaspoon salt
1 tablespoon cornstarch
2 tablespoons vegetable oil

COMBINE SOY SAUCE, rice vinegar, and green onion in small serving bowl. Heat vegetable and chili oils in small saucepan until hot and sizzling; immediately pour into soy-sauce mixture.

Thoroughly combine shrimp with salt in colander placed in sink and let stand for 1 minute. Rinse shrimp under cold running water; drain very well but do not pat dry.

Thoroughly combine shrimp with cornstarch in small bowl, then stir in 1 tablespoon oil; set aside to marinate for 30 minutes or up to 6 hours, covered, in refrigerator.

Heat 1 tablespoon oil in large nonstick skillet or pre-heated wok over high heat. When hot, add shrimp and stir-fry for 2 minutes or just until cooked through. Transfer to small platter and serve with dip. Serves 2 as a main course with rice, 4 to 6 as an appetizer.

GINGER SHRIMP

¾ pound raw shrimp,
  peeled and deveined
1 teaspoon salt
1 tablespoon cornstarch
2 tablespoons vegetable oil
1 large garlic clove,
  chopped

1 tablespoon finely
  chopped fresh ginger
1 large whole green onion,
  chopped
Scant ¼ teaspoon salt
1 tablespoon fresh lemon
  juice

THOROUGHLY COMBINE shrimp with salt in colander placed in sink and let stand for 1 minute. Rinse shrimp under cold running water; drain very well but do not pat dry.

Thoroughly combine shrimp with cornstarch in small bowl, then stir in 1 tablespoon oil; set aside to marinate for 30 minutes or up to 6 hours, covered, in refrigerator.

Heat 1 tablespoon oil in large nonstick skillet or preheated wok over high heat. When hot, add shrimp and stir-fry for 2 minutes or just until cooked through. Add garlic, ginger, green onion, and salt and toss for 1 minute or until tender. Remove from heat and stir in lemon juice. Serves 2 as a main course with rice, 4 with other dishes.

W*hat I like best about this stir-fry is how such simple ingredients – fresh ginger, green onions, a dash of lemon – give the shrimp such a wonderful flavor with so little effort.*

Fresh ginger and a generous sprinkling of salted black beans adds robust flavor to this snappy entrée. ◆ Many recipes suggest leaving the shell on, but I prefer to remove it to allow the shrimp to become permeated with the deliciously pungent ingredients. The shell is usually left on to ensure the shrimp don't dry out, so please be careful: only cook them just until cooked through. ◆ Pimentos are available in supermarkets in glass jars.

SHRIMPS WITH BLACK BEANS

1 pound raw shrimp, peeled and deveined
1 teaspoon salt
1 tablespoon cornstarch
2 tablespoons vegetable oil
2 large garlic cloves, chopped
1 tablespoon finely chopped fresh ginger
1 tablespoon salted black beans, chopped (not rinsed)

1 large whole green onion, cut into 1-inch pieces
2 tablespoons diced pimentos
½ teaspoon sugar
½ teaspoon salt
1 tablespoon dry sherry

THOROUGHLY COMBINE SHRIMP with salt in colander placed in sink and let stand for 1 minute. Rinse shrimp under cold running water; drain very well but do not pat dry.

Thoroughly combine shrimp with cornstarch in small bowl, then stir in 1 tablespoon oil; set aside to marinate for 30 minutes or up to 6 hours, covered, in refrigerator.

Heat 1 tablespoon oil in large nonstick skillet or preheated wok over high heat. When hot, add shrimp and stir-fry for 2 minutes or just until cooked through. Add garlic, ginger, black beans, green onion, and pimento and toss for 1 minute or until tender. Sprinkle with sugar and taste for seasoning, adding salt only if necessary. Splash in sherry and toss for several seconds to combine. Serves 2 as a main course with rice, 4 with other dishes.

BLACK PEPPER SHRIMP

2 tablespoons vegetable oil
¾ pound raw shrimp,
　peeled, deveined, and
　patted dry
1 large garlic clove,
　chopped
1 teaspoon cracked black
　pepper

1 large whole green onion,
　finely chopped
1 teaspoon sugar
1 tablespoon Thai fish
　sauce

HEAT OIL in large nonstick skillet or preheated wok over high heat. When hot, add shrimp and stir-fry for 2 minutes or just until cooked through. Add garlic, pepper, and green onion; toss for 30 seconds. Sprinkle with sugar, add fish sauce, and toss for another 30 seconds. Serves 2 as a main course with rice, 4 with other dishes.

Combining black pepper and briny shrimp creates an easy, exuberant main course. ◆ Cracked black pepper is available in the supermarket's spice section, or make your own by carefully crushing black peppercorns with a mortar and pestle until very coarsely ground.

Not a Cantonese sweet-and-sour dish, but a Thai one. They differ slightly – Thai's use their ubiquitous fish sauce to give fullness of flavor to their sauce – the Cantonese, of course, use soy sauce. But don't substitute soy sauce for fish sauce in this recipe – it just won't work.

SWEET AND SOUR SHRIMP

2 tablespoons unsweetened
  pineapple juice
3 tablespoons ketchup
1 tablespoon sugar
1 tablespoon Thai
  fish sauce
2 tablespoons vegetable oil
¾ pound raw shrimp,
  peeled, deveined, and
  patted dry

2 large garlic cloves,
  chopped
1 tablespoon finely
  chopped fresh ginger
½ teaspoon hot red pepper
  flakes
1 large whole green onion,
  chopped

COMBINE PINEAPPLE juice, ketchup, sugar, and fish sauce in small bowl.

Heat oil in large nonstick skillet or preheated wok over high heat. When hot, add shrimp and stir-fry for 2 minutes or just until cooked through. Sprinkle with garlic, ginger, red pepper flakes, and green onion and toss for 30 seconds. Restir pineapple-juice mixture and add to pan, stirring for 45 seconds to allow shrimp to absorb flavors and become lightly glazed. Serves 2 as a main course with rice, 4 with other dishes.

LEMON GARLIC SHRIMP

1 pound raw shrimp, peeled and deveined	1 tablespoon rice vinegar
1 teaspoon salt	1 teaspoon Japanese sesame oil
1 tablespoon cornstarch	4 large garlic cloves, chopped
2 tablespoons vegetable oil	¼ teaspoon hot red pepper flakes
2 tablespoons sugar	
Grated zest of 1 medium lemon	
3 tablespoons fresh lemon juice	

THOROUGHLY COMBINE shrimp with salt in colander placed in sink and let stand for 1 minute. Rinse shrimp under cold running water; drain very well but do not pat dry.

Thoroughly combine shrimp with cornstarch in small bowl, then stir in 1 tablespoon oil; set aside to marinate for 30 minutes or up to 6 hours, covered, in refrigerator.

Combine sugar, lemon zest, lemon juice, rice vinegar, and sesame oil in small bowl.

Heat 1 tablespoon oil in large nonstick skillet or preheated wok over high heat. When hot, add garlic and red pepper flakes and cook for several seconds or until fragrant. Add shrimp and stir-fry for 2 minutes or just until cooked through. Restir lemon-juice mixture, pour into pan, and toss for 1 minute to glaze and to allow shrimp to absorb flavors. Serves 2 as a main course with rice, 4 with other dishes.

Shrimp are the perfect match for this citrusy and sweet – not to mention garlicky – sauce. ◆ Once, when I demonstrated this simple stir-fry on television, the host was flabbergasted when she realized it wasn't chopped almonds I was adding to my wok, but a copious amount of garlic! Needless to say, she was absolutely enchanted with the end result.

Chinese in technique, Italian in inspiration, this attractive dish demonstrates how easy it is to adapt other cuisines to the stir-fry method. I simply modified one of my own pasta creations by omitting the noodles, adding some shrimp, and then tossing it all up together in my wok.

SHRIMP WITH THREE PEPPERS, CAPERS, AND BASIL

3 tablespoons olive oil
4 large garlic cloves, chopped
¼ teaspoon hot red pepper flakes
⅓ cup diced sweet red pepper
⅓ cup diced sweet yellow pepper
⅓ cup diced sweet green pepper

1 pound raw shrimp, peeled, deveined, and patted dry
2 tablespoons drained tiny capers
¼ teaspoon salt
Freshly ground black pepper
1 teaspoon dried basil
2 cups fresh basil leaves, coarsely chopped

HEAT OIL in large nonstick skillet or preheated wok over high heat. Add garlic and red pepper flakes and cook for a few seconds or until fragrant. Add red, yellow, and green peppers and stir-fry for 30 seconds or until crisp-tender. Add shrimp and toss for 2 minutes or just until cooked through. Sprinkle with capers, salt, pepper, and both dried and fresh basil; toss for several seconds and serve at once. Serves 2 as a main course with rice, 4 with other dishes.

COCONUT SHRIMP WITH GREEN BEANS

2 tablespoons vegetable oil
½ pound green beans, trimmed, cut in half crosswise, then cut in half lengthwise
1 large garlic clove, chopped
1 tablespoon finely shredded fresh ginger

Grated zest of 1 medium lime
½ teaspoon hot red pepper flakes
¾ pound raw shrimp, peeled, deveined, and patted dry
¼ teaspoon salt
½ cup Thai coconut milk

HEAT OIL in large nonstick skillet or preheated wok over high heat. When hot, add green beans, garlic, ginger, lime zest, and red pepper flakes and stir-fry for 1 minute. Add shrimp and salt and toss for another minute or until shrimp are lightly colored on both sides. Add coconut milk, then *constantly* toss for 2 minutes or until shrimp and beans have absorbed most of the coconut milk. (It's important to toss continually for this amount of time to allow the ingredients to fully absorb the coconut flavor. So don't be tempted to let up too early – your wrist will be tired, I know – but it'll be well worth the effort!) Serves 2 as a main course with rice, 4 with other dishes.

*E*xquisitely flavored, shrimp and green beans are stir-fried in coconut milk, ginger, and lime zest until the voluptuous sauce permeates the seafood and beans.
♦ *Serve with Jasmine rice (page 66).*

Limes

CLAMS WITH BLACK BEAN SAUCE

M y urbane rendering of clams with black beans is special: it can be prepared in advance. ♦ For a more conventional version – with the clams left in shells – simply steam and drain them, then stir-fry the opened clams in the oil and aromatic seasonings for 1 minute. Restir the oyster-sauce mixture, add to pan, and stir until sauce slightly thickens. Serve in large bowl garnished with green onion.

2 pounds littleneck clams,
   scrubbed
¾ cup water
2 tablespoons oyster sauce
1 tablespoon cornstarch
1 tablespoon vegetable oil
1 large garlic clove, finely
   chopped

2 teaspoons finely chopped
   fresh ginger
1 teaspoon salted black
   beans, finely chopped
   (not rinsed)
Chopped green onion
   for garnish

PLACE CLAMS in large heavy saucepan and add about ¼ inch water. Cover, bring to a boil, and steam over high heat for 4 minutes or until clams open. Drain, discarding any unopened shells. When cool enough to handle, remove top of each shell and arrange attractively on a heatproof platter. Set aside, or refrigerate if not using immediately.

Using small, sharp knife, remove clams from bottom shells and place in bowl, discarding shells. The clams can be prepared up to this point, covered, and kept chilled.

Combine water, oyster sauce, and cornstarch in small bowl.

Heat oil in large heavy saucepan or preheated wok over high heat. When hot, add garlic, ginger, and black beans and stir-fry for 1 minute or until tender. Restir oyster-sauce mixture, add to pan, stirring until sauce slightly thickens. (The sauce can be done ahead, too, and kept chilled.)

To serve, place platter in 250°F oven for 5 minutes or until shells are heated. Gently reheat sauce, add clams, and cook only until heated through or clams will toughen. Remove platter from oven, spoon clams out of sauce into shells. Divide sauce over clams, sprinkle with green onion and serve at once. To eat, pick up a shell and devour clam and sauce in one delicious slurp! Serves 2 as a main course with rice, 4 as an appetizer.

RICE & NOODLES

◆ ◆ ◆

Fragrant long-grain rice from Thailand, called Jasmine or Fragrant Rice, is available in Asian grocery stores and some supermarkets. If unavailable, you may substitute Basmati – another scented rice from India – or any long-grain rice. ◆ Asians never add salt to rice – preferring its blandness as a counterpoint to highly seasoned dishes and sauces. Salt does bring out more flavor though, so feel free to add it if you wish. ◆ Rice is difficult to make in less than 2 cup amounts: I always make fried rice (see index) with any leftovers.

JASMINE OR WHITE RICE

2 cups Jasmine or long-grain rice	3 cups water
	1 teaspoon salt if desired

PLACE RICE in colander and rinse under cold running water, swishing it around with your hands, until water runs fairly clear; drain well. Place in heavy medium saucepan, add water and salt if desired; bring to a boil over high heat. Cover, reduce heat to medium-low, and simmer for 20 minutes or until rice is tender. Serves 4.

NOTE: There's no exact rice-to-water ratio – it depends on the age of the rice (older takes more water) – and the shape of the saucepan. My recipe is for aged rice. If you get gluey grains, remove the cover for a minute, then replace and continue cooking until the excess moisture has evaporated. Use 1 cup less water with the *same* rice next time and keep trying until you find the winning formula!

CURRIED FRIED RICE

2 skinless, boneless chicken breast halves, cut into ¼-inch thick strips
1 tablespoon water
1 tablespoon cornstarch
¼ teaspoon salt
3 tablespoons vegetable oil
2 tablespoons Thai red curry paste
2 tablespoons Thai fish sauce
2 large garlic cloves, chopped
1 tablespoon finely chopped fresh ginger
1 medium onion, chopped
4 cups cold cooked rice
2 teaspoons sugar
¼ cup coarsely chopped fresh coriander leaves
¼ cup coarsely chopped fresh basil leaves

COMBINE CHICKEN with water in small bowl, thoroughly stir in cornstarch and salt, then 1 tablespoon oil; set aside to marinate for 30 minutes or up to 24 hours, covered, in refrigerator.

Combine curry paste and fish sauce in small bowl.

Heat 1 tablespoon oil in large nonstick skillet or pre-heated wok over high heat. When hot, add chicken and stir-fry for 3 minutes or until opaque and cooked through; remove to plate.

Add remaining oil, garlic, ginger, and onion; stir-fry for 1 minute or until tender. Stir in curry-paste mixture and cook for several seconds or until fragrant. Add rice, breaking up any lumps with hands before adding. Return chicken to pan, sprinkle with sugar, coriander, and basil; continue tossing for several seconds or until heated through. Serves 4 to 6.

R*ice is one of the most versatile grains in the world and fried rice the most versatile rice dish imaginable. The ingredients are so infinitely variable, I bet I could write a cookbook devoted entirely to fried-rice combinations. Red curry paste is a hot and spicy Thai condiment available in Asian markets: don't substitute curry powder in this recipe. ◆ Omit the chicken if you would prefer a simplified version.*

C hock-full of crunchy green things – celery, green pepper, snow peas, peas, and green onions – this rice looks lovely with its all-green vegetables entwined in the pale-colored grain.

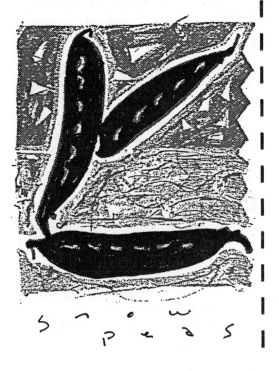

EMERALD FRIED RICE

2 tablespoons vegetable oil
2 large garlic cloves, chopped
1 tablespoon finely chopped fresh ginger
1 medium-small rib celery, cut into julienne
½ sweet green pepper, seeded and diced

10 snow peas, trimmed and cut into julienne
½ cup fresh or frozen peas
3 whole green onions, shredded
4 cups cold cooked rice
½ teaspoon salt
½ teaspoon sugar
2 tablespoons oyster sauce

HEAT OIL in large nonstick skillet or preheated wok over high heat. When hot, add garlic, ginger, celery, and green pepper; stir-fry for 30 seconds. Add snow peas, peas, and green onion and toss another 30 seconds. Add rice, breaking up any lumps with hands before adding, and continue tossing for 1 minute or until heated through. Sprinkle with salt and sugar, add oyster sauce and continue tossing for several seconds or until combined. Serves 4 to 6.

BACON, EGG, AND TOMATO FRIED RICE

1 tablespoon plus
    1 teaspoon vegetable oil
	½ cup tiny fresh or frozen
	    green peas

2 large eggs, well beaten	4 cups cold cooked rice
½ cup diced bacon strips	1 teaspoon salt

3 large whole green onions,
    chopped
	1 cup coarsely chopped
	    ripe, seeded tomatoes

2 large garlic cloves, chopped	2 tablespoons soy sauce
1 tablespoon finely chopped fresh ginger	

HEAT 1 TEASPOON OIL in large nonstick skillet or pre-heated wok over high heat. When hot, add eggs, tilting pan to distribute into thin pancake and cook just until set. Flip over and cook a few seconds to set other side. Transfer to cutting surface and cut into ¼-inch wide strips.

Cook bacon until crisp in large nonstick skillet or pre-heated wok over high heat; remove to plate, leaving bacon fat in pan. Add 1 tablespoon oil; when hot, add green onions. garlic, ginger, and peas; toss for 30 seconds. Add rice, breaking up any lumps with hands before adding, and continue tossing for 1 minute or until heated through. Stir in salt, tomatoes, and egg strips until combined, then soy sauce. Sprinkle with bacon and toss until combined. Serves 4 to 6.

ice is eminently receptive to almost any ingredient. This recent creation of mine – stir-fried rice with crisp bacon, egg ribbons, and tomatoes – is a perfect example. It's great tasting and an ideal accompaniment to many other stir-fries.

Fried rice came into being as a way to use leftovers. This truly flavorsome rendition, combining fresh chiles, basil, and coriander, is a far cry from those humble beginnings. ♦ For more substantial fare, some bite-size pieces of cooked chicken, pork, or shrimp may be added. ♦ The fresh chiles I use here are about 4- to 5-inches long and a little less than ½-inch thick – not the tiny, 1-inch devilishly hot ones.

FRIED RICE WITH BASIL AND CHILES

2 tablespoons vegetable oil
3 large garlic cloves, chopped
1 small onion, chopped
2 fresh red chiles, chopped
4 cups cold cooked rice
1 tablespoon sugar

1 tablespoon Thai fish sauce
1 tablespoon soy sauce
¾ cup coarsely shredded fresh basil leaves
½ cup coarsely chopped fresh coriander leaves

HEAT OIL in large nonstick skillet or preheated wok over high heat. When hot, add garlic, onion, and chiles; stir-fry for 1 minute or until tender. Add rice, breaking up any lumps with hands before adding. Stir in sugar, fish sauce, and soy sauce and toss until heated through. Sprinkle with basil and coriander, toss until combined, and serve at once. Serves 4 to 6.

Shiitake Mushroom Fried Rice

2 tablespoons vegetable oil
¼ cup chopped white onion
2 large garlic cloves,
  chopped
1 tablespoon finely
  chopped fresh ginger
5 medium-small Chinese
  dried black mushrooms,
  soaked in hot water for
  30 minutes, caps thinly
  sliced (¼ cup)

2 small tree ears, soaked in
  hot water for 20 minutes,
  knobby parts removed,
  and thinly sliced (¼ cup)
4 cups cold cooked rice
1 teaspoon salt
½ teaspoon sugar
2 tablespoons oyster sauce

HEAT OIL in large nonstick skillet or preheated wok over high heat. When hot, add onion, garlic, and ginger; stir-fry for 1 minute or until tender. Add mushrooms and tree ears and toss a few seconds. Add rice, breaking up any lumps with hands before adding. Sprinkle with salt, sugar, and oyster sauce and stir-fry for 1 minute or until heated through. Serves 4 to 6.

A *robust, earthy-flavored rice combining Chinese black mushrooms and tree ears. Try it – you'll like it – fried rice never tasted so fabulous!*

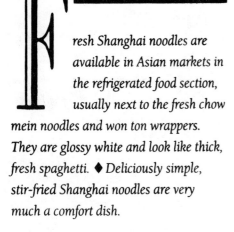

Fresh Shanghai noodles are available in Asian markets in the refrigerated food section, usually next to the fresh chow mein noodles and won ton wrappers. They are glossy white and look like thick, fresh spaghetti. ◆ Deliciously simple, stir-fried Shanghai noodles are very much a comfort dish.

SHANGHAI SOFT-FRIED NOODLES WITH OYSTER SAUCE

½ pound fresh Shanghai noodles
½ teaspoon Japanese sesame oil
2 tablespoons water
2 tablespoons oyster sauce
¼ teaspoon salt
2 teaspoons soy sauce
½ teaspoon sugar
2 tablespoons vegetable oil
1 tablespoon finely shredded fresh ginger

2 large whole green onions, shredded
½ cup matchstick-size strips Chinese barbecued pork
4 small Chinese dried black mushrooms, soaked for 30 minutes in hot water, squeezed dry, caps thinly sliced
1 cup fresh bean sprouts (not rinsed)

COOK NOODLES in large pot of boiling water for 2 minutes; drain well and toss with sesame oil to prevent sticking.

Combine water, oyster sauce, salt, soy sauce, and sugar in small bowl.

Heat oil in large nonstick skillet or preheated wok over high heat. When hot, add ginger, green onions, pork, mushrooms, and bean sprouts and stir-fry for a few seconds or until fragrant. Add noodles, restir oyster-sauce mixture and add, tossing for several seconds or until noodles are heated through and lightly glazed. Serve at once. Serves 2 as a main course with rice, 4 with other dishes.

SCALLION NOODLES

6 ounces dried Japanese
  udon noodles
1 teaspoon Japanese
  sesame oil
1 tablespoon vegetable oil
1 large garlic clove,
  chopped

1 tablespoon finely
  chopped fresh ginger
4 large whole green onions,
  shredded
2 tablespoons oyster sauce

COOK NOODLES in large pot of boiling water for 3 minutes or until al dente; drain, rinse under cold water to remove starch, and drain again. Toss with sesame oil to prevent sticking.

Heat oil in large nonstick skillet or preheated wok over high heat. When hot, add garlic, ginger, and green onions; stir-fry for 30 seconds or until green onion is just wilted. Add noodles and oyster sauce, toss for 1 minute or until heated through. Serves 4 to 6.

*S*callion sounds far more fetching than plain old ordinary green onion, don't you think? ◆ This is a simple tumble of Japanese udon noodles and green onions flavored with ginger and earthy oyster sauce – a pleasing accompaniment to many main-dish stir-fries.

KOREAN NOODLES

One of my favorite Korean recipes, <u>chap chae</u>, is an intriguingly textured dish of bean thread noodles, thin sirloin slices, crunchy vegetables, and toasted sesame seeds. ◆ Serve with rice – Koreans prefer medium-grain rice – steaming cups of barley tea, and – if you live near a Korean grocer – pick up an assortment of pungent <u>kim chee</u> (preserved vegetables) to serve on the side. ◆ I use the largest openings of a 4-sided grater to prepare the carrot and zucchini.

½ pound boneless top sirloin, trimmed and thinly sliced across the grain into 2-inch long strips
1 tablespoon soy sauce
1 teaspoon Japanese sesame oil
¼ teaspoon sugar
3 ounces bean thread (cellophane) noodles
2 tablespoons soy sauce
2 tablespoons Japanese sesame oil
1 tablespoon sugar
⅛ teaspoon salt
2 tablespoons vegetable oil

1 medium onion, thinly sliced
2 garlic cloves, finely chopped
1 medium carrot, shredded
1 medium zucchini, unpeeled and shredded
2 whole green onions, shredded
1 medium tree ear, soaked in hot water for 20 minutes, knobby part removed, and thinly sliced
1 cup fresh bean sprouts (not rinsed)
2 tablespoons lightly toasted sesame seeds

COMBINE MEAT with soy sauce, sesame oil, and sugar in small bowl. Soak bean thread noodles in hot water for 10 minutes (no longer), drain, and cut into 3-inch lengths with scissors.

Combine soy sauce, sesame oil, sugar, and salt in small bowl.

Heat oil in large nonstick skillet or preheated wok over high heat. When hot, add beef and stir-fry for 1 minute or until medium-rare; remove to plate. Add onion and stir-fry for 1 minute or until tender. Toss in garlic, carrot, zucchini, green onions, tree ear, and bean sprouts. Return beef and any juices to pan, then stir in bean thread noodles. Restir soy-sauce mixture and add, then sprinkle with half of the sesame seeds, tossing for 1 minute or until sauce is absorbed. Transfer to warmed platter, and garnish with remaining sesame seeds. Serves 3.

THREE MUSHROOM NOODLE TOSS

3 medium bok choy stalks,
  trimmed
1 cup thinly sliced carrot
6 ounces dried Japanese
  udon noodles
1 tablespoon plus
  1 teaspoon vegetable oil
⅓ cup water
2 tablespoons oyster sauce
¼ teaspoon salt
¼ teaspoon sugar
1¼ teaspoons cornstarch
¼ teaspoon Japanese
  sesame oil

2 large garlic cloves,
  chopped
5 Chinese dried black
  mushrooms, soaked for
  30 minutes in hot water,
  squeezed dry, caps thinly
  sliced
1 cup drained canned straw
  mushrooms, sliced in
  half if large
¾ cup thinly sliced fresh
  white mushrooms

BLANCH BOK CHOY and carrots for 3 minutes in large pot of boiling water; retain boiling water and plunge vegetables into ice water to chill, then drain. Add noodles to boiling water and cook for 3 minutes or until al dente; drain and rinse under cold water to remove starch, and drain again. Toss noodles with 1 teaspoon oil to prevent sticking. Cut bok choy into ½-inch x 3-inch long strips.

Combine ⅓ cup water, oyster sauce, salt, sugar, cornstarch, and sesame oil in small bowl.

Heat 1 tablespoon oil in large nonstick skillet or preheated wok over high heat. When hot, add garlic, the three mushrooms, bok choy, and carrot and stir-fry for 1 minute or until heated through. Add noodles, restir oyster-sauce mixture and add to pan; toss for 30 seconds or until combined and glazed. Transfer to platter and serve. Serves 3 as a main course with rice, 4 with other dishes.

don noodles combined with woodsy shiitake mushrooms, slippery-textured straw mushrooms, and good old button mushrooms create a mushroom lover's delight. ◆ Japanese udon noodles are available in Japanese and Korean markets. ◆ Bok choy is now available in many supermarkets and of course Asian grocers. To prepare bok choy, cut off and discard the root end and tough leaf tops, leaving just a small amount of greens at the top of the white stems.

sweet
red pepper

VEGETABLES

♦ ♦ ♦

Many Chinese recipes incorrectly direct the cook to remove watercress stems before cooking, but it's the crisp stems that the Chinese (and non-Chinese) relish when stir-fried. ♦ I use a salad spinner to remove excess moisture from the watercress after washing, then I place them on clean dish towels and pat dry. Too much moisture results in watery watercress.

STIR-FRIED WATERCRESS

1 tablespoon oyster sauce
1 tablespoon Thai fish
  sauce
1 teaspoon sugar
½ teaspoon cornstarch

2 tablespoons vegetable oil
2 large garlic cloves,
  chopped
2 large bunches watercress,
  well rinsed and dried

COMBINE OYSTER SAUCE, fish sauce, sugar, and cornstarch in small bowl.

Heat oil in large nonstick skillet or preheated wok over high heat. When hot, add garlic and cook a few seconds. Add watercress and stir-fry for 2 minutes or until leaves are wilted and stems crisp-tender. Restir oyster-sauce mixture and add to pan, tossing for several seconds or until greens are lightly glazed. (If there is more than a scant amount of liquid in bottom of pan, transfer greens to serving dish with slotted spoon and boil liquid until slightly thickened; drizzle over greens.) Serves 2 to 4.

Sweet and Sour Cabbage

1½ tablespoons sugar
1 tablespoon soy sauce
1½ tablespoons rice vinegar
1 teaspoon Japanese sesame oil
½ teaspoon salt
¾ teaspoon cornstarch
2 tablespoons vegetable oil
1 large garlic clove, chopped

¼ teaspoon hot red pepper flakes
½ teaspoon Szechuan peppercorns
½ pound very coarsely grated red or green cabbage
1 medium carrot, coarsely grated

COMBINE SUGAR, soy sauce, rice vinegar, sesame oil, salt, and cornstarch in small bowl.

Heat oil in large nonstick skillet or preheated wok over high heat. When hot, add garlic, red pepper flakes, and peppercorns and cook for a few seconds. Add cabbage and carrot and toss for 1 minute or until crisp-tender. Restir sugar mixture and add to pan, tossing for a few seconds to combine. Serve immediately. Serves 4.

Stir-frying shredded cabbage in a faintly sweet-and-spicy sauce produces a delectably crisp and fresh-tasting vegetable. ◆ *Don't overcook!*

R *apidly tossed vegetables glazed with oyster sauce is an easy, simple side dish.*

CARROT, SNOW PEA, AND RED PEPPER STIR-FRY

1 tablespoon vegetable oil
1 cup thinly sliced carrots
1 tablespoon water
20 snow peas, trimmed and sliced in half lengthwise
1 small sweet red pepper, seeded and cut into ½-inch squares

2 large garlic cloves, chopped
1 tablespoon finely chopped fresh ginger
¼ teaspoon sugar
¼ teaspoon salt
1 generous tablespoon oyster sauce

HEAT OIL in large nonstick skillet or preheated wok over high heat. When hot, add carrots and toss for 1 minute. Add water, cover immediately, and cook for another minute, stirring occasionally. Remove cover, add snow peas, red pepper, garlic, and ginger and stir-fry for 1 minute 30 seconds or until crisp-tender. Sprinkle with sugar and salt, then stir in oyster sauce, and toss several seconds or until lightly glazed. Serves 2 to 4.

SPINACH WITH BROWNED GARLIC

2 tablespoons vegetable oil	1 teaspoon dry sherry
4 to 6 large garlic cloves, coarsely chopped	½ teaspoon sugar
	¼ teaspoon salt
10 ounces fresh spinach (not frozen), well rinsed and dried	1 teaspoon cornstarch mixed with 2 teaspoons water

HEAT OIL in large nonstick skillet or preheated wok over high heat. When hot, add garlic and cook for several seconds or until browned but not burnt. Add spinach, standing back in case of spattering, and stir-fry for 1 minute or until limp. Splash in sherry; toss and sprinkle with sugar and salt.

Restir cornstarch mixture and add to pan, tossing to combine. Transfer spinach to small platter, arranging some of the browned garlic on top. Serves 2 to 4.

sually, garlic is not supposed to be browned, but here, the lightly charred fragrant bulb is the perfect complement to spinach.

Simple ingredients, yet simply delish. ◆ A very hot pan is essential to create those flavorful little charred bits on the vegetables – what Chinese chefs call wok fragrance.

SNOW PEAS WITH GREEN ONIONS

1 tablespoon vegetable oil
½ pound snow peas,
   trimmed

3 large whole green onions,
   shredded
¼ teaspoon salt

HEAT OIL in large nonstick skillet or preheated wok over high heat. When hot, add snow peas and green onions and stir-fry for 30 seconds or until crisp-tender. Sprinkle with salt and toss until combined. Serves 2 to 4.

CHINESE EGGPLANTS
WITH BLACK BEAN SAUCE

¼ cup chicken broth
1 tablespoon oyster sauce
½ teaspoon sugar
½ teaspoon salt
1 teaspoon cornstarch
¼ cup vegetable oil
2 Chinese eggplants
   (¾ pound), unpeeled,
   stem ends removed,
   cut lengthwise into 8ths,
   then cut in half crosswise
2 large garlic cloves,
   chopped

1 tablespoon finely
   chopped fresh ginger
1 tablespoon salted black
   beans, chopped
   (not rinsed)
½ teaspoon hot red pepper
   flakes
2 tablespoons diced
   pimento
1 large whole green onion,
   cut into 1-inch pieces

COMBINE CHICKEN BROTH, oyster sauce, sugar, salt, and cornstarch in small bowl.

Heat oil in large nonstick skillet or preheated wok over high heat. When hot, add eggplant and stir-fry for 5 minutes or until tender and lightly charred. Sprinkle with garlic, ginger, black beans, red pepper flakes, pimento, and green onion and toss for 1 minute or until tender. Restir chicken-broth mixture and add to pan, tossing for a few seconds or just until lightly glazed. Serves 2 to 4.

ere again, the zippy embellishment of black beans, ginger, and garlic make this dish a standout. ♦ Until recently, Drew and I had to eat at our favorite Chinatown restaurant to satisfy our cravings for this eminently appealing dish but, happily, I've fashioned my own deeply delicious devise to serve hot from my own wok. ♦ Long, thin Chinese eggplants with pale purple skins are a must – regular eggplant can't be substituted. Chinese eggplants are available at Asian markets and some specialty greengrocers. ♦ Pimentos are available in supermarkets in glass jars.

E

ggplant with zucchini and red pepper is a classic combination in Italian cuisine. ♦ I've used regular eggplant here because they're more commonly available, but it's preferable to use small Italian or Japanese eggplants which don't require pre-salting to remove bitterness. ♦ It's also a good idea to use a nonstick skillet rather than a wok, otherwise you might need to add more oil.

EGGPLANT, ZUCCHINI, AND RED PEPPER STIR-FRY

1 pound eggplant, unpeeled, ends trimmed and sliced into ½- × 4-inch strips
1½ teaspoons salt
About 3 tablespoons olive oil
2 large garlic cloves, chopped
1 medium-large zucchini, trimmed, unpeeled and sliced into thick julienne
1 medium sweet red pepper, seeded and cut into thick julienne
Pinch salt
Freshly ground black pepper
1 tablespoon butter
1 cup fresh basil leaves, coarsely chopped

TOSS EGGPLANT and salt in large colander; set in sink to drain for 30 minutes. Pat slices dry with paper towels.

Heat 1 tablespoon oil in large nonstick skillet or preheated wok over high heat. When hot, add eggplant and stir-fry for 3 minutes, adding a little more oil if necessary. Add garlic and continue tossing eggplant for 2 more minutes or until every slice is tender; remove to plate.

Add another tablespoon oil and zucchini and stir-fry for 1 minute or just until tender; remove to plate with eggplant.

Add remaining tablespoon oil and red pepper and stir-fry for 1 minute or until crisp-tender. Return eggplant and zucchini to pan and sprinkle with salt and pepper. Stir in butter and basil and toss for several seconds until combined. Serves 4 to 6.

Celebrate the arrival of asparagus with this splendidly crisp complement to any Asian meal, or serve the asparagus as an appetizer.

STIR-FRIED ASPARAGUS WITH OYSTER SAUCE

2 tablespoons vegetable oil
2 large garlic cloves, chopped
1 pound slender fresh asparagus, well rinsed, tough ends snapped off, and cut into 2-inch pieces

1 tablespoon Thai fish sauce
2 tablespoons oyster sauce
1 teaspoon sugar

HEAT OIL in large nonstick skillet or preheated wok over high heat. When hot, add garlic and asparagus and stir-fry for 1 minute or until crisp-tender. Stir in fish sauce, oyster sauce, and sugar and continue tossing for 30 seconds or until nicely glazed. Serves 4.

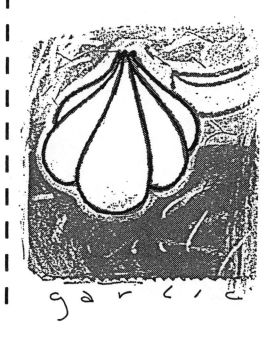

garlic

avory oyster sauce is perfectly suited to enrich and enhance vibrant green broccoli florets.

BROCCOLI WITH OYSTER SAUCE

2 tablespoons vegetable oil
2 large garlic cloves, chopped
1 bunch broccoli florets and small stems only, cut into bite-size pieces

2 tablespoons chicken broth
2 tablespoons oyster sauce
1 teaspoon sugar

HEAT OIL in large nonstick skillet or preheated wok over high heat. When hot, add garlic and broccoli and stir-fry for 30 seconds. Add chicken broth and quickly cover pan; cook for 1 to 2 minutes, stirring frequently, until broccoli is tender but still bright green. Remove cover, stir in oyster sauce and sugar and continue tossing until lightly glazed. Serves 2 to 4.

HOT AND SPICY GREEN BEANS

¾ pound green beans,
 trimmed
1 tablespoon vegetable oil
2 large garlic cloves,
 chopped

1 tablespoon finely
 chopped fresh ginger
1 tablespoon chili paste
 with soy bean
½ teaspoon salt

BLANCH BEANS in boiling water for 4 minutes or until tender but still bright green (don't undercook – the beans must be tender and not too crisp for the correct texture); plunge beans into ice water to chill, then drain. Pat dry with paper towels. (The beans can be prepared ahead up to this point, covered, and refrigerated until using.)

Heat oil in large nonstick skillet or preheated wok over high heat. When hot, add garlic and ginger; cook for a few seconds. Add beans, chili paste, and salt and stir-fry for 1 minute or until beans are coated and flavored with seasonings. Serves 2 to 4.

Typically, these spicy Szechuan beans are deep-fried until they become wrinkled and bright green. I've lightened my recipe by blanching the beans in boiling water, which not only reduces calories and fat, but also creates a much simpler version. The beans may not have that funky wrinkled appearance, but they taste just as terrific.

*O*nce again, oyster sauce – that wonderful Chinese condiment – adds its distinctive richness to a simply delicious stir-fry. Cutting the beans in half lengthwise is a little tedious, but the actual cooking takes merely a minute.

STIR-FRIED GREEN BEANS WITH OYSTER SAUCE

2 tablespoons vegetable oil
2 garlic cloves, chopped
1 whole green onion, shredded
1 tablespoon finely chopped fresh ginger

¾ pound green beans, trimmed and cut in half lengthwise
½ teaspoon salt
1 generous tablespoon oyster sauce

HEAT OIL in large nonstick skillet or preheated wok over high heat. When hot, add garlic, green onion, and ginger and cook for a few seconds. Add green beans and salt and stir-fry for 1 minute or until beans are crisp-tender. Add oyster sauce, toss for a few seconds more or until beans are glazed. Serve immediately. Serves 2 to 4.

ITALIAN GREEN BEANS AND MUSHROOM STIR-FRY

½ pound green beans, trimmed
2 tablespoons olive oil
1 large garlic clove, chopped
¼ pound fresh white mushrooms, thinly sliced
Salt
Freshly ground black pepper
¼ cup freshly grated Parmesan cheese

BLANCH BEANS in boiling water for 4 minutes or until tender but still bright green (don't undercook – the beans must be tender and not too crisp for the correct texture); plunge beans into ice water to chill, then drain. Pat dry with paper towels.

Heat oil in large nonstick skillet or preheated wok over high heat. When hot, add garlic and green beans and stir-fry for 30 seconds or until heated through. Add mushrooms and continue tossing for 1 minute or until mushrooms are just cooked through. Sprinkle with salt, pepper, and Parmesan cheese; immediately remove from heat and stir until combined. Serves 2 to 4.

N*eedless to say, this Italian-inspired invention of flash-fried green beans and mushrooms tossed with Parmesan cheese makes a smashing vegetable course. ◆ The beans can be blanched, chilled in ice water, and drained, then covered and refrigerated several hours ahead. Bring back to room temperature before proceeding.*

Q uickly-fried zucchini enlivened with a liberal dash of aromatic herbs is a pleasing accompaniment to any non-Asian meal.

♦ Sprinkle with thyme for a French accent or basil for Italian.

ZUCCHINI STIR-FRY WITH THYME OR BASIL

4 medium zucchini (about 1½ pounds), unpeeled
1 teaspoon salt
1 tablespoon vegetable oil

½ teaspoon dried thyme or basil
Freshly ground black pepper

RINSE ZUCCHINI well and trim ends. Cut zucchini into julienne using a mandoline (a professional vegetable cutter) or sharp knife. Toss with salt in colander and place in sink to drain. Set aside for 20 minutes, then take small handfuls of zucchini and squeeze out excess moisture. Pat dry with paper towels.

Heat oil in large nonstick skillet or preheated wok over high heat. Add zucchini, thyme or basil, and pepper. Stir-fry for 2 minutes or until crisp-tender; do not overcook. Serve at once. Serves 2 to 4.

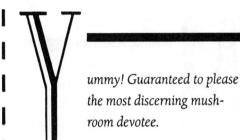

ummy! Guaranteed to please the most discerning mushroom devotee.

TWO MUSHROOMS WITH SESAME SEEDS

1 tablespoon vegetable oil
1 tablespoon butter
½ teaspoon Japanese sesame oil
½ pound fresh white mushrooms, thinly sliced
8 medium Chinese dried black mushrooms, soaked for 30 minutes in hot water, squeezed dry, caps thinly sliced

2 tablespoons toasted sesame seeds
1 tablespoon oyster sauce

HEAT OIL, butter, and sesame oil in large nonstick skillet or preheated wok over high heat. When hot, add white mushrooms and stir-fry for 1 minute or just until beginning to brown. Add Chinese mushrooms and sesame seeds; toss for 30 seconds and stir in oyster sauce until lightly glazed. Serves 2 to 4.

My meatless version of the popular Szechuan stir-fry known as Ma Po's Pork and Bean Curd is as simple as it is satisfying.

HOT AND SPICY TOFU

5 tablespoons chicken broth
1 tablespoon hot bean sauce
1 teaspoon sugar
1 teaspoon mushroom soy sauce
1 tablespoon cornstarch
2 tablespoons vegetable oil
2 large garlic cloves, chopped

1 tablespoon finely chopped fresh ginger
1 large whole green onion, chopped
1 pound drained bean curd, cut into 1-inch cubes
1 teaspoon Japanese sesame oil

COMBINE CHICKEN BROTH, hot bean sauce, sugar, soy sauce, and cornstarch in small bowl.

Heat oil in large nonstick skillet or preheated wok over high heat. Add garlic, ginger, and green onion and toss for several seconds or until fragrant. Add bean curd and gently stir-fry for 1 to 2 minutes or until heated through. Restir chicken-broth mixture, add to pan, drizzle with sesame oil, and stir until lightly glazed. Serves 2 as a main course with rice, 4 with other dishes.

 INDEX

◆ ◆ ◆